ANGUS FAIRHURST

ANGUS FAIRHURST

SACHA CRADDOCK
WITH JAMES CAHILL

PWP
IN ASSOCIATION WITH
Sadie Coles HQ
LONDON

© 2009 Sadie Coles HQ

All works © The Estate of Angus Fairhurst

First published in 2009 on the occasion of the exhibition, Angus Fairhurst,
at Arnolfini, 16 Narrow Quay, Bristol BS1 4QA www.arnolfini.co.uk, by

Sadie Coles HQ
35 Heddon Street, London, W1B 4BP/
69 South Audley Street, London, W1K 2QZ
www.sadiecoles.com

Philip Wilson Publishers
109 Drysdale Street, The Timber Yard, London, N1 6ND
www.philip-wilson.co.uk

Distributed throughout the world
(excluding North America) by:
I.B.Tauris & Co. Ltd
6 Salem Road, London, W2 4BU

Distributed in North America by:
Palgrave Macmillan, a division of St Martin's Press
175 Fifth Avenue, New York, NY 10010

ISBN: 978-0-85667-659-8 (hardback)
ISBN: 978-0-85667-660-4 (paperback)

Edited by Pauline Daly, Rebecca Heald and Katy Reed

Designed by Keith Pointing

Printed in China by Everbest

Front cover image: *A Couple of Differences between Thinking and Feeling II*, 2003
Back cover image: detail of *Fata Morgana*, 2008

Title page: *An Effortless Patch #1*, 1998

Marcel Duchamp *Étant donnés: 1. la chute d'eau / 2. le gaz d'éclairage,* 1946–66
© Succession Marcel Duchamp/ADAGP, Paris and DACS, London 2008
Photograph: Philadelphia Museum of Art: Gift of the Cassandra Foundation, 1969
Samuel Palmer *The Magic Apple Tree*, 1830 © Fitzwilliam Museum,
University of Cambridge, UK/The Bridgeman Art Library

CONTENTS

Foreword
Nicholas Serota 7

Infinite Possibility and Variety
Metaphor, Methodology and Influence
in the Art of Angus Fairhurst
James Cahill

Corpus 11

Apostrophes 13

Otherness 18

Reduction 20

Edges 24

Giving and Taking Away
Sacha Craddock

Fata Morgana 31

Lowest Expectations 49

A Couple of Differences between Thinking and Feeling 67

Underdone/Overdone Paintings 91

Magazine, All Body and Text Removed 107

Acknowledgements 137

Biography 138

Full List of Works 141

MY HOUSE FELL DOWN BUT NOW I CAN SEE THE STARS

A fairhurst 01

My House Fell Down but Now I Can See the Stars, 2001

Angus Fairhurst: Confounding Expectations

It is going to be a while before we can fully comprehend the fertile mind and anarchic spirit of Angus Fairhurst. Angus didn't make it easy, either for himself or for his audience. He deflected enquiries, appeared to be making great deviations from the path, and switched frequently from one medium to another, moving fluently between painting, collage, sculpture, animation, the computer, performance and, forever, drawing. Most critics, curators, collectors and camp-followers of his generation saw his work infrequently in large mixed exhibitions. They could not follow the thread in an oeuvre that includes works of great beauty and sensuousness as well as some in which violence and frustration come to the fore. Nor could they understand how such passions were so frequently touched by a gentle, ironic humour. Was this really one artist at work?

Fairhurst denied himself the comfort of making signature art, and with it the safety of a conventional career. There were, nevertheless, consistencies that ran through his thinking and the making of his work. Most obvious was his affection for and exploration of collage. His obsession with layering, both physical and conceptual, and with the silhouette, developed through the *Underdone/Overdone* paintings of the mid-nineties to the small collages and billboard works of later years. From the earliest grey paintings shown in Freeze in 1988, his works are richly sensuous in their feeling for material, suggestive in their abstraction and frequently sensual in their exploration of the contour of the body.

However, he also had an innate feeling for colour, from the primaries of the *Low, Lower and Lowest Expectations* series to the rich oranges, pinks and greys seen in the paintings, silk-screens and collages of his final show. The palette in these late works reminds me of Francis Bacon's early paintings, especially *Three Figures at the Base of a Crucifixion*. In these same late works, the billboards, advertising signs and blank walls of faceless buildings evoke the common, shared, but often hostile and dangerous, spaces of the inner city urban experience.

As an artist, Fairhurst had a fondness for laying down images, one upon another, to the point where illegibility gives way to new meaning. Seemingly dull repetition can often reveal deeper truths. In one of his sound pieces, Bruce Nauman endlessly repeats the words 'THANK YOU' until this expression of gratitude becomes menacing, threatening and uncomfortably close to the expletive 'FUCK YOU.' Like Nauman, or Beckett for that matter, Fairhurst's apparently dull repetition, seen in his paintings and performances of the mid-nineties, translates into the rhythms and entropy of life. Expectation is dashed, but hope may surface in survival as the rituals of life continue. One of his drawings shows four pillars in surrounding blackness, *My House Fell Down, but Now I Can See the Stars*. All hope is not lost.

A haunting quality distinguishes much of his work. His images distil the contemporary worlds of advertising, billboards, and magazines, and lodge themselves in our memories more insistently than their sources, so that the languor of Sophie Dahl will live longer in the Fairhurst painting than in the original Opium perfume advertisement. All this is achieved with a light touch and a deceptively simple gesture that opens a new perspective on a familiar world.

Angus himself had a similar elegance. Purposeful without being over-bearing, he had a way of quietly putting and then gaining his point. His drawings convey a wistful, elegiac humour. The gorilla contemplates his image in the pool or regards his detached arm lying on the ground. And a mythical (or is it pantomime?) animal with the head remarkable inventions by an artist whose humour and ideas will tease and stretch our imagination for many years into the future? There is so much still left for us to explore in the work of Angus Fairhurst.

Nicholas Serota
Director, Tate
May 2008

Unseen, 2004

Infinite Possibility and Variety
Metaphor, Methodology and Influence in the Art of Angus Fairhurst

JAMES CAHILL

Angus Fairhurst (1966–2008) trained at Goldsmiths College, London. He was one of the central figures of what became universally known as the YBA (Young British Artists) phenomenon of the 1990s. While at Goldsmiths in 1988, he participated in and (along with Damien Hirst) helped to organise the group exhibition Freeze. This now legendary show presented work by sixteen Goldsmiths contemporaries, including Sarah Lucas, Mat Collishaw and Gary Hume. Fairhurst went on to be exhibited in a number of key surveys of British art – Some Went Mad, Some Ran Away in 1994; Brilliant! New Art from London in 1995; Apocalypse in 2000; and In-A-Gadda-Da-Vida – a joint show with Hirst and Lucas – in 2004.

Throughout his career, Angus Fairhurst's output remained inexhaustibly innovative and multidirectional. Employing a wide variety of media – from performance and animation to painting and bronze casting – Fairhurst's themes embraced questions of metaphor, artifice and repetition; these often found expression via tense dialectical oppositions. Despite his varied practice, a number of works stand out as singular icons – depictions of the English forest, images made through a persistent process of reduction, and gorillas.

Corpus

A giant gorilla crouches in contemplation before its own detached arm. This tragicomic spectacle in bronze, *A Couple of Differences between Thinking and Feeling II* (2003; p. 81), expresses some of the dichotomies at the heart of Angus Fairhurst's art – the cerebral and the emotional, the sublime and the absurd, the familiar and the alien. The fragmented body scrutinising itself is also an apt analogy for Fairhurst's artistic corpus. Encompassing bronze gorillas, multilayered magazine collages, computer-drawn patterns transcribed in paint, anthropomorphic cartoons, pastoral silk-screens, and the late canvases and sculptures that compress many of his divergent impulses, Fairhurst's art is defined by its elusive heterogeneity.

In its breadth of styles and mercurial slippages in tone, Fairhurst's output mirrors the plurality of British art in recent decades. It traverses the figurative concerns of the School of London and the collaborative experiments of the underground scenes of the eighties and nineties.[1] At different points, Fairhurst made paintings that evoke the sparse realms of Francis Bacon's triptychs, and devised music and video performances that dismantle the very distinction between artist and artwork.

His work's historical sentience is manifested in its emulation of the appropriative strategies of Dada, which it harnesses to the Conceptualist principles of the sixties and seventies (in particular the Poststructuralist notion of the de-centred subject). At numerous moments it reaches further into art history, assuming a *longue durée* perspective.[2] But ultimately, Fairhurst's disparate undertakings point back to a highly individual system of reference.

Through an oeuvre spanning twenty years from his time at Goldsmiths (1986–89) to his death in March 2008, visual and conceptual tropes run back and forth in an oscillation of prolepsis and echo. Instances of this can be traced on several levels. A figure in a gorilla suit holding up its own detached head, one of Fairhurst's early sketched vignettes of gorillas in absurd scenarios, reappears ten years later in epic-scale bronze (pp. 74 and 87). It is one of several such metamorphoses where cartoonish slapstick fossilises into darker humour tinged with pathos. Methodological concepts are subject to similar transmutations. The progression towards a monochrome 'absolute' shown in *Low, Lower and Lowest Expectations* (1996–97; pp. 48–65) – where Op-Art-style patterns mass together ever more densely in each painting – reemerges in the *Underdone/Overdone Paintings* (1998; pp. 90–105), at odds with the works' Romantic pastoral subject matter of interlocking trees.

Fairhurst actively dramatised the interconnections between his works. The hall of mirrors, a vehicle of infinite repetition, tellingly forms the subject of many pieces, whether in the Baroque ripples of *Imagine You Are Top Banana* (2000) or the bathetic *Banana Skin in the Hall of Mirrors* (2000) – a fake banana skin inside a cardboard box lined with mirrors. Fairhurst conjured up a hall of mirrors again in *Pala02* (2007; p. 35).

Here, within a fictive arena where perspective lines zoom towards multiple vanishing points, the zigzagging planes of fragmented advertisements echo each others' forms and are themselves partly reflected in a pool-like ellipse.

Fairhurst once more underlined the resonances between his works with his curatorial practices. For his exhibition Dysuniversal in 2004, he juxtaposed a sculpture named *Unseen* – another mirrored pool – with wallpaper derived from the earlier *Underdone/Overdone Paintings*. Contained within mottled bronze banks, the pool picked up the imagery of Fairhurst's earlier work (itself in mediated, reproduced form) both literally and generically. At the same time, the conceit glanced back at the English pastoral tradition of John Constable and Samuel Palmer.[3] So art history glimmers spectrally in Fairhurst's work at the same time as the work repeats itself and playfully spells out its own repetitions, with the result that his art is almost akin to an allegory of Postmodern re-presentation.

In his catalogue text for Freeze in 1988, Ian Jeffrey articulates a distinctively Postmodern sense of history: 'Once upon a time there were completely new starts, with yesterday a long way off, but under the new terms of reference the present comes less as itself than as the recent past redone, re-recorded, or maybe never even away.'[4] This view of the present in terms of a not-yet-historicised past, and of the past and present flowing almost indiscernibly into each other, presciently encapsulates an important aspect of Fairhurst's outlook. His artistic corpus may be regarded, then, as a variegated *gesamtkunstwerk*, subtly woven through with key thematic and theoretical threads.

Apostrophes

Just as Fairhurst's artistic corpus comes close to an allegory of Postmodern methodology, many of his works are underscored by ideas of metaphor and substitution. A number of early pieces consist of photographs punctured with plastic clothing tags. The photographs were initially lifted from postcards and magazines; later, Fairhurst began using his own – for instance in *Man with Dream Colours* (1992; p. 95), four tag-riddled images in which a young man, seated and suited, holds up a square canvas in a series of different colours.

Fairhurst likened the plastic tags to 'physical apostrophes that have taken on their own life…They stand in for that whole consumer/producer angle, like an apostrophe does for a letter. Thousands of them together look like a mass of little marks that have created a new word.'[5] The squares in *Man with Dream Colours* perform a similar metaphoric function, perhaps standing for the emptiness of commercial promises (why are the colours 'dream colours'?), or the way in which supposedly unique items can be glibly substituted.

The concept of visual apostrophes lies behind Fairhurst's cut-out and collaged advertisements, produced prolifically from around 2003, where outlines and blanks are used to imply an original whole (pp. 112–36). These have their roots in his earlier postcard sets *All Evidence of Man Removed* and *All Evidence of Man Blacked-In*, and his pages of magazines with all the graphics and areas of text excised, as in *Faces – All Text & Graphics Removed* (2000; p. 111). Fairhurst later began layering the hollowed-out sections of pages on top of one another in increasing layers, using not only magazines,

Three Double Pages from a Magazine, Body and Text Removed, 2004

Rainbow's End (inside), 2000

but bus-stop and billboard adverts (pp. 126–29 and 122–25). In *Three Double Pages from a Magazine, Body and Text Removed* (2004), for example, the shape of a reclining female is filled out by areas of white and fragments of underlying imagery. Her outline becomes a window into another realm, her stiletto boots slicing through the surface illusion of a sofa in a room.

In this way, Fairhurst deconstructs the metonymic images of adverts – beautiful bodies, luxuriant interiors – to reveal their intrinsically incomplete and substitutive nature. Yet paradoxically, his technique extends the process by which visual advertising itself selects, excises and dissimulates, so as to recast reality in a shorthand or metalanguage of paradigms.

A close antecedent of Fairhurst's advertisement works is *Rainbow's End* (2000), which is folded in half to create a front 'cover' showing Peter Blake's iconic *Babe Rainbow*

Marcel Duchamp Étant donnés: 1. la chute
d'eau / 2. le gaz d'éclairage, 1946–66

design. Inside, amid a montage of found photographs redolent of Blake's Pop-Art assemblages, a naked and sunned female body sprawls out with Lilliputian farm animals mounted around and on top of her. To the right is a graphite drawing of a free-floating pelvis and colon surrounded by mirrors. The incongruous elements of the work come to appear like apostrophes for Fairhurst's own enduring preoccupations. The drawing of the colon intimates cyclical processes, as explored in his early animation loops; the strips of globular 'cells' from a Chuck Close painting instance the deconstruction of an image into its constituent elements – the guiding principle behind the collages and his works in prime colours, *Low, Lower and Lowest Expectations* and *Underdone/Overdone Paintings*; and the mirrors imply unremitting self-reflexivity, as evidenced by his continual translation and retranslation of his own artistic idioms.

In their massing together of metaphors, *Rainbow's End* and the subsequent collages bear revealing similarities to Marcel Duchamp's celebrated project *Étant donnés* (1946–

66).[6] Viewed through peepholes in wooden doors is a model of a female body, her head concealed from view, reclining in a luminous landscape. The realism of the scene is undercut by the figure's skewed anatomy and indeterminate genitalia (Duchamp built the mannequin for *Étant donnés* from a number of differently angled plaster casts of his lover's body, resulting in a conflation of perspectives). Abnormal anatomies, mainly in the form of disembodied arms and legs, also appear in many of Fairhurst's drawings and animations. In a sequence from *Things That Don't Work Properly/Things That Never Stop* (1998), a swivel chair spins to reveal a figure with alternating male and female genitals, before the rotation speeds up and the images are superimposed to create a hermaphroditic jumble. The fragmentary phantasms of Fairhurst's collages are correspondingly multidimensional and allusive: the outline of the woman in *Ten Pages from a Magazine, Body and Text Removed* (2007; p. 130) forms a compendium of multiple poses, angles, objects and places.

Underlying Fairhurst's notion of substitution – of the part standing for an unseen, and perhaps unattainable, whole – is an attitude of inadequacy, a sense of both his own shortcomings as an artist and those of artistic representation per se. This stance, evoked by just such a title as *Things That Don't Work Properly/Things That Never Stop*, again calls to mind Duchamp, who once coyly professed, in an almost Eubulidean liar paradox, that 'everything I am telling you now is stupid and wrong.'[7] Fairhurst communicates a wry

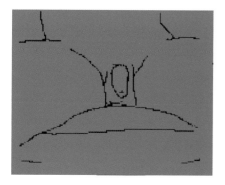 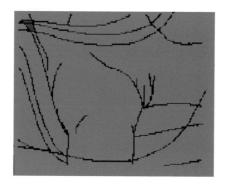 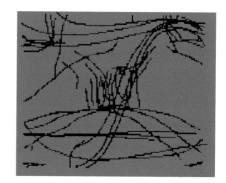

Stills from Things That Don't Work Properly/Things That Never Stop, 1998

sense of the ever-present risk of being 'stupid and wrong' most succinctly in *Banana Skin in the Hall of Mirrors*, a work that represents an infinity of potential slip-ups.

Fairhurst's semi-serious preoccupation with failure also informs his numerous acts of 'blockage'. His works frequently foreground their own artifice and play out their limitations. In *Portugal-Drilled* (1996; p. 106), a postcard riddled with drill holes, Fairhurst sabotages the original image to leave us with a fragmentary, impressionistic remnant that, like a decayed ancient parchment, draws attention to the inevitable incompleteness of art (and indeed all cultural records). He revealingly described the plastic tags on his early pieces as acting 'in two ways: they may push you away, but first they draw you in, or the other way round…interrupting the progress of the image.'[8] Duchamp's wooden doors performed precisely the same kind of interruption, at once enticing and holding back the viewer. Whether in the tag pieces, drilled works, or the multiple elisions of his collages, we repeatedly see Fairhurst disrupting the 'progress of the image' in order to illumine the seemingly unbridgeable gulf between representation and interpretation, as well as that between the signifier and signified.

Otherness

Allegory, literally meaning 'speaking [something] other', is one of many manifestations of 'otherness' in Fairhurst's art. Each artistic style is explicitly 'other' relative to the last; his works conjure forth 'other' realities; and on occasion he cast himself as someone or something 'other', or de-centred himself altogether.

A prime instance of this tactic of self-displacement was the employment of amanuenses to make the *Low, Lower and Lowest Expectations* paintings, each series of which was formed of 'twelve paintings made by drawing them on a computer and giving the results to a sign writer to paint in enamel on aluminium panels.'[9] The use of surrogate practitioners, of course, has immediate precursors in conceptual artists as divergent as Sol LeWitt and Martin Kippenberger (the latter's panoply of styles closely anticipates Fairhurst's art as a whole).[10]

Fairhurst shared their Modernist aim of 'authorial impersonality'. Yet his deliberate interjection of several stages between the works' conception and completion (the initial action with a computer mouse, printing the patterns out, copying the printouts onto aluminium) also evinces a necessary paradox of art making – the subsuming of disjointed stages of transmission into a finite work, and the consequent 'otherness' of artistic product from imaginative origin.

In the figure of the gorilla, Fairhurst shadows forth man's animal 'other'. Bestial yet approximate to the human form, he identified gorillas as inherently anthropomorphic: 'Gorillas are a useful image because they're very close to the human shape, so you can draw them doing human activities without having to characterize or personalize them. They represent a certain kind of thing in mankind.'[11] The emergence of the gorilla motif in his art can be traced back to a show of his drawings and cartoons at Sarah Lucas's London flat in 1994.[12] In these, gorillas appear in surreal human situations – surfacing from a brimming bath smoking a cigarette or force-feeding liquor through a funnel to a dummylike man. From around the turn of the millenium, Fairhurst began making sombre bronze successors to the cartoons – *A Couple of Differences between Thinking and Feeling* (2000; p. 66), *A Couple of Differences between Thinking and Feeling II* (2003; p. 81), and *Untitled* (2007; p. 76).

At times, the gorilla becomes a stand in for Fairhurst himself, his imaginative other. This kind of self-projection has numerous parallels, notably in Duchamp's ventriloquial alter ego Rrose Sélavy. In *A Cheap and Ill-Fitting Gorilla Suit* (1996) (also the title of a video from the previous year), a furry costume is stuffed with newspaper so as to appear to recline in contemplation; one almost imagines a pensive Fairhurst within. In *Pietà* (1996; p. 89), however, a photograph of Fairhurst as the dead Christ in the lap of a fake gorilla, the gorilla becomes his prop as opposed to his understudy. In contrast to his self-displacements elsewhere, Fairhurst is the central, naked subject of *Pietà*. And so, at different junctures, Fairhurst could be said both to affirm and reject Roland Barthes's 'Death of the Author' discourse, albeit in visual rather than literary terms.

Fairhurst attributed the pathos of his gorilla scenarios to a further kind of otherness – 'a discrepancy between many idealised things and their everyday reality.'[13] The same discrepancy holds between Michelangelo's *Pietà* and Fairhurst's reworking on a studio couch, or between a real gorilla and the cheap and ill-fitting suit. An early drawing of a gorilla with a detached hand (or glove) seems to imply that everything is ultimately mimetic. In this cartoon, Fairhurst paraphrases a theory, stretching back to Plato, that all visible objects are imperfect representations: material bodies are flawed copies of invisible, eternal Forms.

Fairhurst's later works conjure stagelike 'other realities' and comprise a *heteroglossia* of other artistic voices. *Pala02* unites the *trompe l'oeil* perspective of a Dürer etching with the gloss and shimmer of a nightclub interior. The smooth-planed worlds of *Saen01* and *Saen02* (2007; pp. 30 and 33) – which contain windows of hollowed out advertisements (compressions of countless 'flawed copies') – convey the virtual reality of computer games. Indeed, Fairhurst designed his late paintings with the help of a computer, using it to set up an otherworldly realm suggestive of multiple, unreal possibilities.

The stark geometrical structures and spare palettes of these and Fairhurst's other late paintings derive from seventeenth-century Dutch church paintings, in particular the works of Pieter Saenredam (1597–1665), whose influence is implicit in the titles.[14] In the foreword to this volume, Nicholas Serota furthermore identifies a resemblance between the late paintings' orange-walled settings and those of Francis Bacon's triptychs. Like the malformed beasts of *Three Studies for Figures at the Base of a Crucifixion* (1944), the sinuous figures of *Fata Morgana* and *Schopfun* (both 2008; pp. 40–41 and 36–37) appear poised between materialisation and dissolution into formlessness. They are at once suggestive of backlit images of the Madonna in church windows and mythological Sirens. Each painting represents a polyreferential labyrinth that invokes the cumulative 'megatext' of western art and so repeatedly summons forth the artistic and cultural 'other'.

Reduction

In its mediation of form and formlessness, reduction is another principal leitmotif in Fairhurst's art. In the collages, context is obliterated to leave behind only the aquiline outlines of the source material. The accumulation of the same banal patterns on top of one another in the *Low, Lower and Lowest Expectations* series entails an eradication of the original forms (zigzags and squiggles occupying ten distinct horizontal bars). But the superimpositions, which begin in the fourth painting of each series, simultaneously engender new, dense masses of colour, which gesture towards a monochrome absolute – an end that could betoken either the apotheosis or the annihilation of form.

This paradox is starkest in *Low Expectations*, where we see a progression towards utter blackness. The last panel in the series recalls Kazimir Malevich's iconic *Black Square* (c. 1923), the embodiment of his Suprematist ideal of 'purely pictorial art'.[15] Malevich equated the absence of objective form with a new, transcendental level of perception: 'the black square on a white background was the first shape used to convey the absence of an object. Society recognised in non-objective representation the end of art but failed to perceive in it the direct body of perception.'[16] More emphatically still, Malevich's Abstract Expressionist successor Ad Reinhardt (also an exponent of the black monochrome) argued that fifty years of abstraction had rendered art 'purer and emptier, more absolute and more exclusive – non-objective, non-representational…'.[17]

Yet, in accordance with his half-ironic stance of falling short or 'underdoing', Fairhurst did not quite achieve the monochrome purity he gestured towards, later remarking: 'I didn't make it to black by the twelfth painting but I reached a point where the variation between one stage and the next had become less visible, and it seemed academic to pursue the absolute.'[18] The elusiveness of that 'absolute', pursued but never arrived at, ultimately points to the artificiality of binary oppositions, whether between the objective and nonobjective, the pure and abject, or the formal and formless.

Low, Lower and *Lowest Expectations* were also the titles of musical performances and albums made by Fairhurst's band Low Expectations from 1995.[19] The group simply mimed to samples of pop songs, knowingly playing up to the charge that contemporary art has simply ripped something else off, that it is the sort of thing one could have done oneself. In later performances, the samples were played over one another in a process of cumulative layering until musical order dissolved into Babelian incoherence. But the expulsion of form could equally signal a Dionysian release, as suggested by the critic Michael Archer, who observed of one of the performers: 'the movements of the girl seem increasingly guided by some inner impulse rather than by sounds around her.'[20]

Fairhurst's series of silk-screens, *Underdone/Overdone Paintings*, embodies an antithesis between accumulation of forms and reduction into formlessness. Fairhurst initially rendered scenes of trees in varying combinations of the three primary colours, as in

Primary Forest 5. He then laid these images over each other at random over a sequence of thirty pictures. Dominant tones occasionally threaten to clog the image (see *Underdone/ Overdone Paintings* nos. 26 and 30, pp. 104-5), resulting in an abstraction akin to the near-blackness of the last painting in *Low Expectations*, which in its dual concentration and bareness could reflect either the 'overdone' or 'underdone' of the title.

This tendency towards abstraction conflicts with the works' Romantic pastoral imagery, based on five photographs of 'blocked views' in Epping Forest. While the reduction of the scene into prime colours presages an ultimate obliteration of recognisable features, it also recalls the selective palettes of Nash, the pre-Raphaelite landscapists and Palmer. The latter's extolment of the 'raving mad splendour of orange twilight glow' could well be applied to a number of the *Underdone/Overdone Paintings*.[21] Indeed, there are striking lines of continuity between the reduced perspective and primacy of colour in *Primary Forest 5* and the Romantic, 'visionary' style of Palmer and his followers, as illustrated by a work such as *The Magic Apple Tree* (1830), a golden-hued idyll framed by boughs.

Primary Forest 5, 1998

Samuel Palmer The Magic Apple Tree, 1830

A related tension exists between the crafted, painterly style of the individual pictures, especially those at the beginning of the series, and their mechanical, Pop-Art style of production and installation in repetitious grid form.[22] Art-historical genres collide within several of the works: fragments of newspaper visible behind the thinner areas of paint constitute a Modernist reassertion of picture surface against pictorial illusion.

Fairhurst's reduction of design or illusion to a state of 'pure' flatness and saturated colour therefore gives rise to a number of uneasy oppositions. Fundamentally, each of these implies the dual occlusion and materialisation of form. This duality reflects Fairhurst's wider interest in the fragile balance between certain generative processes and their negatives, as expressed in an early interview where he identified the body as a site of simultaneous reduction and increase: 'The body, in a lifetime, is constantly replacing old cells with new ones in order to stop the degeneration of the whole tissue.'[23]

Edges

Fairhurst's art is underpinned by an acute awareness of edges, borders and thresholds. He once revealingly stated that 'You have to keep on trying to make things and show their edges. The edge becomes the important part, the part that allows people in…a big part of artmaking in the 20th century has been about showing the edge, about removing artifice, removing illusion. It's the edge of dissimulation, if you like.'[24]

Fairhurst equated showing the 'edge of dissimulation' to 'seeing the back of the canvas', in other words, to perceiving the threshold between reality and illusion. In *The Truth in Painting*, Jacques Derrida persuasively argues that the picture frame, an equivalent threshold, acts in the same way as a parergon (an object that is secondary or supplementary to the main work), so as to 'touch [the artwork], push it, press it, press against it, seek contact, exert pressure at a frontier.'[25] It serves not as a barrier, but as a hinge that both separates everything extrinsic to the work and connects the work with the exterior world, facilitating a discourse between the work's interior and exterior.

The bus-stop signs within *Fata Morgana* and *Schopfun* act as a metaphor for this idea of the border as a hinge – the site of discourse between interior and exterior – as well as that of the uncertainty of imposed edges. Their oblong outlines disintegrate haphazardly to allow in sections of the background arena, and the hollowed out sections become 'frames' in their own right, containing and qualifying the exterior space. At the same time, the evanescent forms of the bus-stop signs threaten to break out into the wider picture: in *Schopfun*, for instance, patches of paint and sections of photograph overrun their prescribed border.

In these final paintings, Fairhurst also emphasises the material surface of the image – the pivotal 'edge of dissimulation' – through a synthesis of blockages and excisions that glance back to earlier projects. In *Fata Morgana, Gree* (2008; p. 44), *Eenp* (2008; p. 45), and *Enpa* (2008; p. 46), semitransparent, pixellated orange and red lines streak across the paintings (in an echo of Fairhurst's transcription of digital forms in *Low, Lower and Lowest Expectations*).[26] At points, they serve almost to deface the picture, occluding its forms in the fashion of scribbles and highlighting Fairhurst's will to obliterate, rub out and redo. Elsewhere, they disappear into the world of the image, either behind a floating column or bus-stop advert.[27] In *Fata Morgana*, trickles and flecks of paint in turn cover parts of the canvas, drawing us inexorably back to the physical surface or 'frontier' of the painting.

The interface between the interior worlds of the paintings and exterior material reality, therefore, is evinced within these paintings through a simultaneous disruption and reinforcement of illusion. This grows out of a conflict between manmade and computerised forms, as well as between deliberate and apparently indiscriminate gestures. Indeed, the stripped-down bus-stop signs combine torn edges with incisions and brushstrokes that seem calculated to preserve a sense of illusion. The former recall the lacerated posters of the Décollage Affichiste artists Jacques Villeglé and Raymond Hains, which contributed to the emergence of Nouveau Réalisme in the 1960s, and lay emphasis on the works' materiality, drawing equally upon Arte Povera and the slashed canvases of Lucio Fontana.[28]

The flickering outlines of the figures within the bus-stop signs also intimate mental thresholds. In its mixture of opacity and transparency, the hollow white figure of *Fata Morgana* – empty except for a flaming line of hair and a misaligned fragment of buttocks – suggests the point at which ocular perception stops and imaginative projection begins. It is a 'blank canvas' both in the sense of being a negation (that is, having much of its detail stripped away) and being a site of myriad potentials. In the same way, the *terrain vague* of *Fata Morgana* and *Schopfun* seems like a blueprint for more choreographed and mannered designs: Fairhurst drew influence for these works not only from paintings of bare Calvinist churches but also from the Villa Borghese in Rome, whose ornate schemata could almost be traced onto the blank façades and diagrammatic floor plans.

The 'edge' is central to Fairhurst's late paintings in terms of the liminal quality of their passageways, bus-stop signs and fragments of collage; all come to symbolise the threshold between the subliminal and the conscious (subliminal effect, of course, being the advertisements' *raison d'être* in their original form).[29] The paintings' cryptic titles also serve to reinforce the sense of half-formulated thoughts on the edge of conciousness – *Schopfun* (perhaps a variant on *Schöpfung*, meaning 'creation'), *Gree*, *Eenp* and *Enpa*.

Furthermore, the collaged forms of *Fata Morgana* and *Schopfun* pointedly mimic the miragelike effect of a scientific fata morgana (where airstreams of different temperatures cause the refraction of objects on the horizon, so that concrete forms become distorted and etherised). The phenomenon is recorded in Werner Herzog's film *Fata Morgana* (1971), the inspiration for Fairhurst's title, which dwells on the barren landscape of a desert before examining sites of wreckage. The chimerical forms and vacant spaces of Fairhurst's final works raise similar questions about the distinction between the authentic and imaginary, and underline the sense of potential that is inherent in any negation – pointing ultimately to the instability of meaning, or the arbitrariness of seemingly fixed definitions.

Dualisms reverberate throughout Angus Fairhurst's work. He expounded in Manichean terms his key notions of metaphor, otherness, reduction and edges, with artifice ranged against reality, accumulation against reduction, and negated space against potential space. These dualisms divert us inexorably towards the other, the parallel, the *parergon*; and, of course, Fairhurst's art often intimates a parallel reality permissive of splits and contradictions where different chains of association link together and 'parallels meet in defiance of geometric law.'[30]

But he also underlined the artifice of over-rigid oppositions, implying their potential to unravel into a multiplicity of meanings, or collapse into meaninglessness. In a lecture in 2004, he enumerated the mass of uneasy, antithetical processes at the heart of his practice:

> It's up there for thinking and down there for dancing. An infinite possibility
> and variety of slipping up, falling over, overreaching, making mistakes;
> underdoing, overdoing; doing, and having to re-do; undoing and remaking;
> hollows and protuberances; suppression and openings; possibilities and denials.
> I'm not qualified. There's been a mistake.[31]

For Fairhurst, art represented an imperfect means of shoring up against 'mistakes', fragmentation or failure, whether on an emotional or academic level. It is this recognition – ever enlivened by his offbeat sleights of hand – that gives his work its deceptive yet enduring power.

Notes

1. A recent illustration of the plurality of British art towards the end of the twentieth century was the exhibition The Secret Public: The Last Days of the British Underground 1978–1988, Institute of Contemporary Arts, London, 23 March–6 May 2007. See also Matthew Collings, *Blimey!: From Bohemia to Britpop: The London Artworld from Francis Bacon to Damien Hirst* (London: 21 Publishing, 1997), 50–54, 58–64 and 92–98. For Fairhurst's collaborative projects with Damien Hirst and Sarah Lucas, see Gregor Muir, 'It Must be a Camel (For Now)' in Gregor Muir and Clarrie Wallis (eds.), *In-A-Gadda-Da-Vida*, exh. cat. (London: Tate Publishing, 2004), 90–92.

2. In *La Méditeranée et le monde méditerranéen à l'époque de Philippe II* (first published 1949), Fernand Braudel seminally advocated the analysis of history under a range of 'magnifications', the most important being the *longue durée*, on the scale of centuries.

3. Dysuniversal, Georg Kargl, Vienna, 10 November–31 December 2004. A similar installation featured in Fairhurst's exhibition Notnot at Vacio 9, Madrid, 14 September–17 October 2005: the sculpture *Bent Pond* reflected itself in its perpendicular mirrors as well as the surrounding wallpaper design. In-A-Gadda-Da-Vida, Tate Britain, 3 March–31 May 2004, again explicated intracorporal resonances as well as proposing parallels between Fairhurst's work and that of Sarah Lucas and Damien Hirst.

4. Ian Jeffrey, *Freeze*, exh. cat. (London: PLA Building, 1988). Fairhurst's work in the show was *Grey Unit*, a grid of subtly variegated grey oblongs. His grid paintings on hardboard included grids of flecks of varnish and drilled holes.

5. Angus Fairhurst in interview with Simonetta Gimella in Gianni Romano (ed.), *Angus Fairhurst*, exh. cat. (Geneva: Galerie Analix, 1992), trans. Guido Ruffino.

6. Duchamp worked in secret on *Étant donnés: 1. la chute d'eau / 2. le gaz d'éclairage* (*Given: 1. The Waterfall / 2. The Illuminating Gas*) from 1946 to 1966. It is regarded as mirroring a number of earlier works, notably *The Large Glass* (1915–23).

7. Marcel Duchamp quoted in William Seitz, 'What's Happened to Art? An Interview with Marcel Duchamp on the Present Consequences of New York's 1913 Armory Show', *Vogue NY*, vol. 141, no. 4, February 15 1963, 113. On the subject, Nikolaus Pevsner amusingly remarked: 'None of the other nations of Europe has so abject an inferiority complex about its own aesthetic capabilities as England.' Pevsner, *The Englishness of English Art* (London: Penguin Books, 1964), 25.

8. Angus Fairhurst in interview with Simonetta Gimella.

9. Angus Fairhurst, 'Angus Fairhurst Talks Film', Tate Britain, 17 April 2004.

10. Gregor Muir interestingly notes that the young Fairhurst displayed work on the walls of Michel Wurtle's Paris Bar, a haunt of Kippenberger's. *In-A-Gadda-Da-Vida*, 90.

11. Angus Fairhurst in interview with Marco Spinelli, London, 11 March 1995, reproduced in Richard Flood (ed.), *Brilliant! New Art from London*, exh. cat. (Minneapolis: Walker Art Center, 1995), 34–35.

12. *In-A-Gadda-Da-Vida*, 92.

13. Angus Fairhurst quoted in Clarrie Wallis, 'In the Realm of the Senseless', *In-A-Gadda-Da-Vida*, 102.

14. Strong parallels can be traced between Fairhurst's late works, *Fata Morgana* and *Schopfun* (both 2008), and Saenredam's *Church of Saint Odulphus, Assendelft* (1655) and *Interior of the Church of St Odulphus at Assendelft, seen from the Choir to the West* (1649), notable for their atypical angles and pronounced geometry.

15. Kazimir Malevich, 'Cubism and Futurism to Suprematism: The New Painterly Realism (1915–16)', reprinted in C. Harrison and P. Wood (eds.), *Art in Theory, 1900–1990* (Oxford: Blackwell, 1992). Quoted in Larissa A. Zhadova, *Malevich, Suprematism and Revolution in Russian Art 1918–1933* (London: Thames & Hudson, 1982), 45. Fairhurst explicitly alluded to Malevich in the ironic homage *Malevich's Grave* (2001), a set of near-black magazine pages with sections cut out to reveal drawings of a hall of mirrors, a bathtub, and other signature Fairhurst motifs.

16. Kazimir Malevich, 'Die gegenstandslose Welt', Bauhaus Bücher II, Munich, 1927, quoted in Zhadova, 50.

17. Ad Reinhardt, 'Art as Art', *Art International*, vol. VI, no. 10, December 1962.

18. Angus Fairhurst, 'Angus Fairhurst Talks Film'.

19. For an extensive analysis of Fairhurst's music, see Jörg Heiser, 'Trivial Pursuit: Low, Lower, Lowest Expectations – Music and Performance in the Work of Angus Fairhurst' in Yilmaz Dziewior (ed.), *The Foundation*, exh. cat. (Kraichtal: Ursula Blicke Stiftung, 1999), trans. Gérard A. Goodrow, 24–27.

20. Michael Archer, 'Theatre of the Absurd' in Norman Rosenthal (ed.), *Apocalypse: Beauty and Horror in Contemporary Art*, exh. cat. (London: Royal Academy of Arts, 2000), 200.

21. G. Grigson, *Samuel Palmer, the Visionary Years* (London: Kegan Paul, 1947), 59. Fairhurst's affinity with the pastoral is also evidenced in the light box photographs *A False Dawn on the Road to Personal and Artistic Freedoms* (1996), where he leaps into the air in a verdant pasture, and in *An Effortless Patch #1–4* (1998), soft focus photographs of him being progressively obscured by blooming flowers.

22. The *Underdone/Overdone Paintings* were first exhibited in The Missing Link, Sadie Coles HQ, London, 28 October–28 November 1998.

23. Angus Fairhurst in interview with Damien Hirst, in Romano (ed.), *Angus Fairhurst*. The statement accords with Fairhurst's repetitious, cyclical system of artmaking and tellingly echoes Roland Barthes's notion of structure expounded through the allegory of the Argonauts' ship, replaced bit by bit 'so that they ended up with an entirely new ship, without having to alter either its name or its form … [the *Argo*] affords the allegory of an eminently structural object'. Barthes quoted in Rosalind E. Krauss, *The Originality of the Avant-Garde and Other Modernist Myths* (Cambridge, Mass., and London: MIT Press, 1985), 2.

24. Angus Fairhurst in interview with Marco Spinelli.

25. Jacques Derrida, *The Truth in Painting* (1978), trans. Geoff Bennington and Ian McLeod (Chicago: University of Chicago, 1987), 55.

26. Fairhurst's translations of computerised forms importantly recall the work of German artist Georg Herold, particularly his 1995 exhibition Compu.comp Virtual Visualities Equivacs Bitmapdys, in which a set of wall-based works made from Mylar mirrors and wooden blocks were joined together to create twisting lines, which imitate the effect of computer pixels.

27. These works were exhibited in Fairhurst's last show, at Sadie Coles HQ, London, 21 February–29 March 2008. The title *Fata Morgana* is taken from Werner Herzog's 1971 film of the same name, which Fairhurst acknowledged as a source of inspiration in his lecture 'Angus Fairhurst Talks Film' (cited above). Herzog's films *Lektionen in Finsternis* (*Lessons in Darkness*, 1992) and *Die Große Ekstase des Bildschnitzers Steiner* (*The Great Ecstasy of Woodcarver Steiner*, 1974) provided the titles of two other works in the show, *Lessons in Darkness* and *The Great Ecstasy* (both 2008).

28. See Benjamin HD Buchloh, 'From Detail to Fragment: Décollage Affichiste', *October*, vol. 56, High/Low: Art and Mass Culture, Spring 1991, 98–110.

29. Interestingly, Threshold was the title of a show by Fairhurst in 2005 (Max Wigram Gallery, London, 24 June–03 Sept 2005), which included a series of framed cut-out magazine works - *Double Page Spread Painting* (2004) – with paint splashed across the glass, once more foregrounding the interface of picture surface and pictorial illusion.

30. M. Riffaterre, *Semiotics of Poetry* (Bloomington: Indiana University Press, 1978), 86.

31. Angus Fairhurst, 'Angus Fairhurst Talks Film', 2004.

Saen01, 2007

Giving and Taking Away

SACHA CRADDOCK

Fata Morgana

Waiting for the bus, near the tree that sprouts, near the trunks that miraculously remain, the outline of a fantasy girl with long hair takes up a mannered pose in a fake situation.

The two large paintings in Fairhurst's recent exhibition at Sadie Coles HQ, *Fata Morgana* and *Schopfun* (both 2008; pp. 40–41 and 36–37), propose layered and complex spatial plans, with evidence included and elements removed. These ambiguous places lie somewhere in the walkway, under- or overground, and suggest a myriad of exits. The flooring, marked out in conflicting geometry, allows the sense of a stage, a gallery for reality.

The bus shelter in *Fata Morgana* represents perpetual limbo, a site for thought, an in-between destination, somewhere but nowhere, with advertising, positioned for subliminal effect, mixing with real context for unconscious thought and association. The muffled blur or whir as the picture shifts up the electronic board makes this a temporary London place for passing thoughts that either hold, or diffuse. But no one, apart from someone who takes conscious note, is actually looking when the image changes.

These paintings mirror an illusory reality, as Fairhurst's concentration is on the perpetual pull between two and three dimensions. The place becomes a moving, albeit broken, frame upon which expectations of future perfection and false desire can come and go. Besides the obvious notion that image is illusion and the real is nonexistent in reproduction, Fairhurst's work has always hovered in between a faith in the perpetuation of the image and an inbuilt awareness of the impossibility of such an endeavour.

The struggle between image and emptiness in Fairhurst's work is reflected in his choice of the title *Fata Morgana*, after Werner Herzog's film of 1971. As much a surprise to the director as it was radical for the audience at the time, the film consists of simple footage of the Sahara desert. It is a moving panorama of natural form and human intervention, with dried-out beasts, broken cars, the colonial legacy of empty buildings, and continual goose-pimpled layers of sand. The excellent score and slow shifts in attention to detail make it a heartbreaking mirage of loss and gain.

Fairhurst's painting entitled *Fata Morgana*, completed very soon before the opening of the show, suggests a state of both innocent construction and deliberate deconstruction. The place depicted is the site for a transition of possibility. The advertising has been stripped away to expose what already exists. But the woman, or girl, with hand archly holding the shopping bag strings in the manner of Galatea in Raphael's fresco in the Villa Farnesina in Rome, is somehow more present in her depleted outline. With her back in kittenish curve and gesture merging phone-booth card with the brass of high street fashion, she becomes a delicious point for painted depth and real reference. A naked, torn, pulled-away presence, she is dependent on Fairhurst's sophisticated references in order to come alive again.

Fairhurst's principle of taking all timely, anecdotal evidence of man away makes for a rather half-empty, half-full redistribution of the quotidian. The photographic detail glimpsed behind the emptied figure is at a different angle, suggesting an apparently bottomless sideways layering. Here, the smudged comet trail of drawing establishes enough interference to undo illusion and make contrast. The woman is part of the scenery in a broken and disordered place, though she is part of a picture she can never really disrupt because it is as if she never really existed.

Fairhurst worked at these paintings from compositions arranged first on the computer but then transcribed onto canvas. The mock-up translated in broad brush shows his continuing love for the process of production, as well as the formative process that confirms that one language does not equate to another. The hand that follows a computer notion cannot help but get lost in material scale, intention, and an endeavour that is so emphatically different. The initial sense of organisation and vision soon unravels to lead somewhere else.

Saen02, 2007

The paintings are traditional in their use of a three-dimensional arena to combine a sense of desire and recognition with the back-slap of contradictory disquiet. But there is the slight tear, the relief of shadow, that makes it clear the inspiration is turning into something else. Fairhurst's tendency to take away until, as he suggests, there is nothing left, means that the process of painting is, in contrast, a matter of making, of adding. To leave it as it was would be to show the ultimate emptiness, but by taking away Fairhurst leaves what might be there, and reveals a faith in the image to reinvent, restore and recreate itself.

Executed with skill and tentative pleasure, these recent paintings betray a constant pull between the point for making something and the way a process can so easily lead away. Fairhurst had said that he worried that the earlier 'Overlapping Paintings' (*Low, Lower and Lowest Expectations* (1996–97; pp. 48–65)) were over-controlled and over-directed, but the difference here is the part that he plays in physical and temporal relation to the paintings.

With this, and other exhibitions, Fairhurst works with the whole impression, the collective way in which media and elements placed together can inform, counterweight and support each other, if only to imply a contradiction. The range of new work is formally clear – Fairhurst never obsessed with adolescent ideas of formal breakdown for its own sake – with two huge paintings, four smaller canvases, a free-standing bronze sculpture on a deep and generous plinth, and a broken, see-through 'for sale' sign mounted on the inside gallery wall.

The tragic bronze tree, a cartoon illustration of free-flowing movement held still, is packed with serious possibility, despite its solid state. The last sculpture, *Lessons in Darkness* (2008; p. 38), which was made with the faintest suggestion of touch and decision to bring out an unusual level of narrative, seems caught in an incident, which is at once happening, is about to happen, and has already happened.

In this work Fairhurst very keenly and openly refers to Bernini's Daphne who is literally turning into a tree as she tries to escape, to run away. The movement seems to will that actual, visual transformation. The speed with which she seems to make her escape is important here because the sculptural object is stationary, a static representation

Pala02, 2007
Overleaf: Schopfun, 2008

of movement and place. Something has happened, with mangled mess of limb and branch, that is at once the beginning, end, and aftermath.

Of the generation that pushed back and forth between interpretation and the artistic futility of message, this exhibition was perhaps reassuring for Fairhurst. When you looked into illusory space, through the easy relationships between elements, past the comment, you reached a source of further questioning.

The small paintings carry exactly the touching melancholy of Nash. The tree drawn in *Eenp* (2008; p. 45) rises up, miraculously and surprisingly, out of the barren ground of the canvas. And yes – and this brings back the bus shelter – trees do survive along the main routes, around Old Street, and the back-lit advertising boards, passed by bus, scooter, or cab, glow to offer what was only circuitously indicated by the see-through brokenness of *The Great Ecstasy* (2008; p. 42), the remade 'for sale' sign at the entrance of Fairhurst's show. Capitalism, weakened, is at the end of solidity.

Above: Untitled (with Bird), 2007
Left: Lessons in Darkness, 2008
Overleaf: Fata Morgana, 2008

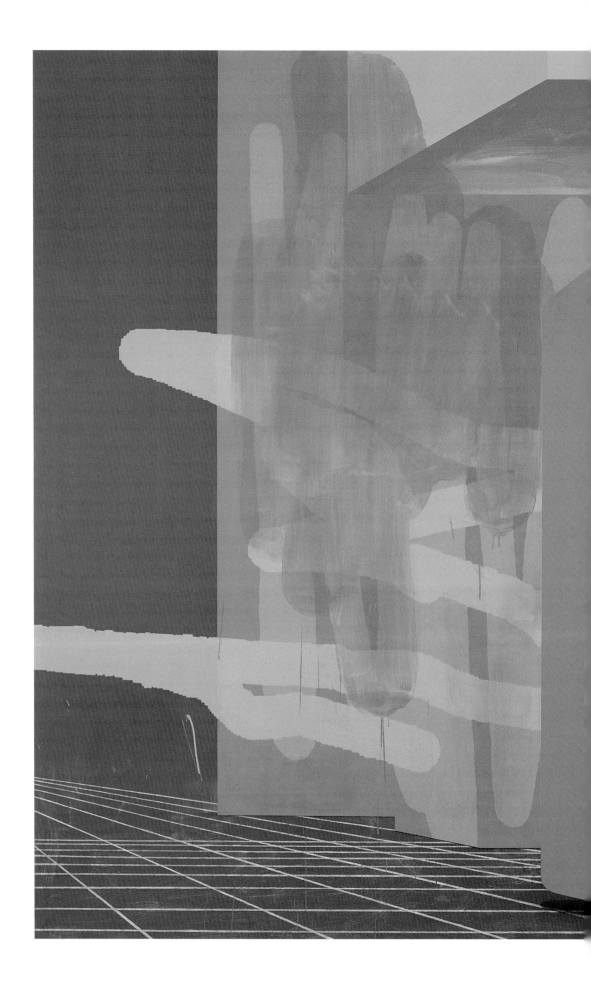

Above: Epha, 2008
Left: the Great Ecstasy, 2008

Gree, 2008

Eenp, 2008

Enpa, 2008

Installation views, Sadie Coles HQ, London, 21 February–29 March 2008

Lowest Expectations

This series of paintings, made by sign writers at Fairhurst's request, shows how meaning can live, unabsorbed, on the surface. The work is caught in a deliberately ambiguous role between painting, collage and photography. Sign writers wrote these paintings, all of them, and they are not physical or intimate in the way paintings can be. 'From sense to no sense to some sense': a doodle based on the human genome has been put into a computer to produce a series of patterns painted in green, red, blue, yellow, black, and white.

Fairhurst's continually evolving miming band, Low Expectations, staged a series of performances starting in 1995. This band, variously made up of Mat Collishaw, Gary Hume, Pauline Daly, Cerith Wyn-Evans, Joe Strummer, Philippe Bradshaw, Nicole Hackert, Chris Bell, Ant Genn and Andrew Hale, among other friends and fellow artists, would construct the musical equivalent of the paintings of the same name. With the continuous repeating of thirty-second loops from the beginnings of ten well-known pop songs, the compositional build up would naturally lead to subsequent breakdown. Layer upon layer of sound would build until structure, song, or score became lost in deafening obliteration. At the same time, Fairhurst's figurative cartoon animations would continually overlay one another and repeat at the back of the stage, reflecting the sound and pushing all towards further oblivion.

The *Low, Lower and Lowest Expectations* paintings, having the appearance of being both separately spectacular and communally intelligible, make some sort of sense while still promising everything that is possible in modern painting. The casual repeat patterns imply movement or sound, radiating out and over to make a rather slow, then fast, implication of speed or noise. There is some separate logic here, in that they are made by sign painters rigorously following instructions. The overlapping gathers momentum until the twelfth painting is almost solid black. Here Fairhurst is, by whatever means, alluding to the natural conclusion in painting towards the 'all over', to the excessive use of a painterly point to make, ultimately, no point.

The language used here is shorthand, a notification of language, a kind of Morse code to be beaten out: dot, dot, dash, dash. It is a notation that looks like it sounds and sounds as it looks.

Left: Detail of 5th Lowest Expectations, 1996

Low Expectations, Performance, 21 Dean Street, London, 26 November 1996

A slow rhythm builds to a dark cacophony. The point perhaps lies elsewhere, in the way that the notation and paint look like a musical score, an illustration of decorative motifs, or an Etruscan detail around a tomb door, all taken far from source by translation and filed in the reference book under title and letter, yet able to make a separate impression nonetheless.

Fairhurst talked of the rules he set up for this series and the ways he would intercept and interlink; the apparent psychological flatness with which he approached its production. It is this flat, disingenuous way of approaching a project that produces an effect so far removed from the fake science with which it had started.

The sign writers worked like Victorian clerks, only as instructed, but the evidence of human error delighted Fairhurst, as such accidents proved that the mechanical appearance of these paintings was, in fact, illusory. In retrospect, Fairhurst certainly admitted a sense of awkwardness to the 'then wilful avoidance of composition'; he worried that he was perhaps over-programmatic about the move away from 'harmony and intentional disingenuity'; he wondered if he should have been so tied to the sequential. But then, Fairhurst's whole working approach can be found in the delicate charm of these paintings. They are visual and anti-visual, formal and informal, but then also, in turn, they show his resulting bafflement after having been inside and outside the production, the process, and its subsequent meaning, a delight and a dilemma.

The *Low, Lower and Lowest Expectations* paintings carry connotations of craft, writing, music, and, most fundamentally to Fairhurst, print. This gathering together of a faintly recognisable sense, this knitting of stylistic hints made by others over generations, produces a lexicon of attitude.

The paintings on their own stop time in the flow of logic. Rather than a series where, old fashioned, the difference is in the nuance of colour, the difference between each of these paintings is in the number of layers, the relation to distance, and the obliteration of the edge. Painted in enamel on aluminium, the signs are the result of an accumulation of a breakdown in meaning. By adding too much information there is a sort of spluttering until 'detail goes, distance goes, and the space behind something goes, and all is black.'

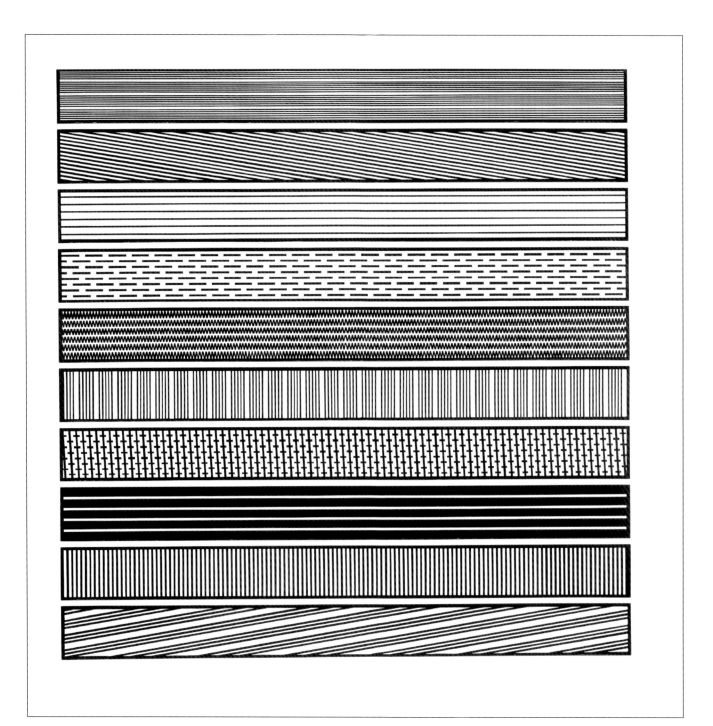

Low Expectations, 1996

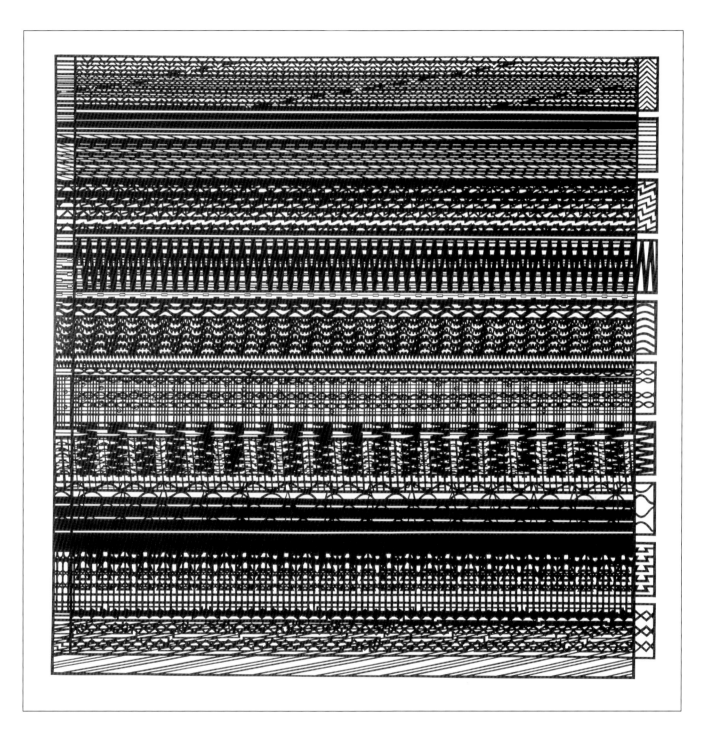

6th Low Expectations, 1997

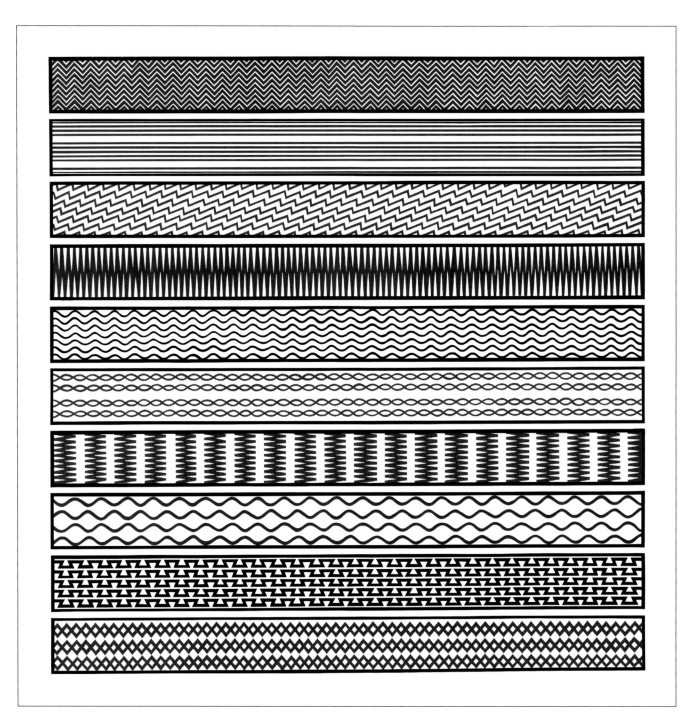

Lower Expectations, 1996

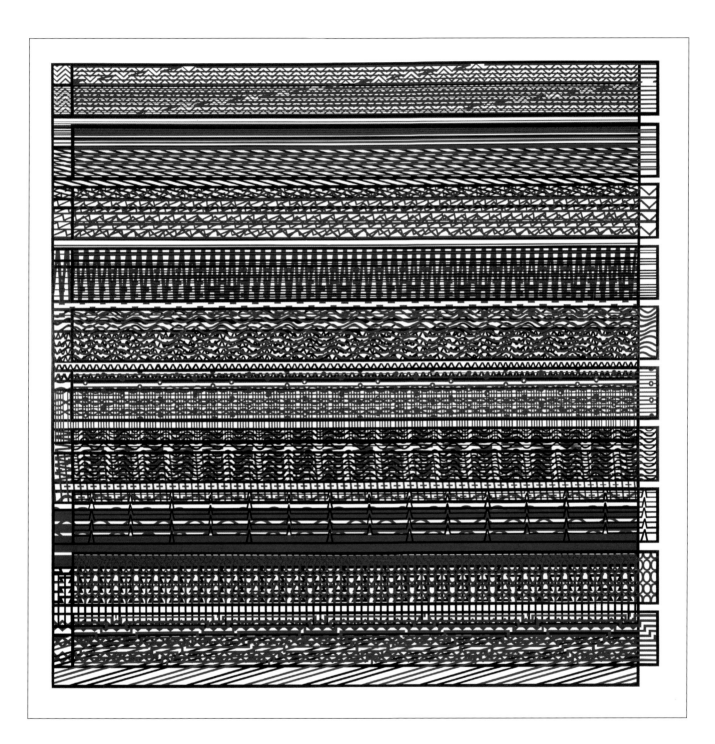

6th Lower Expectations,1997

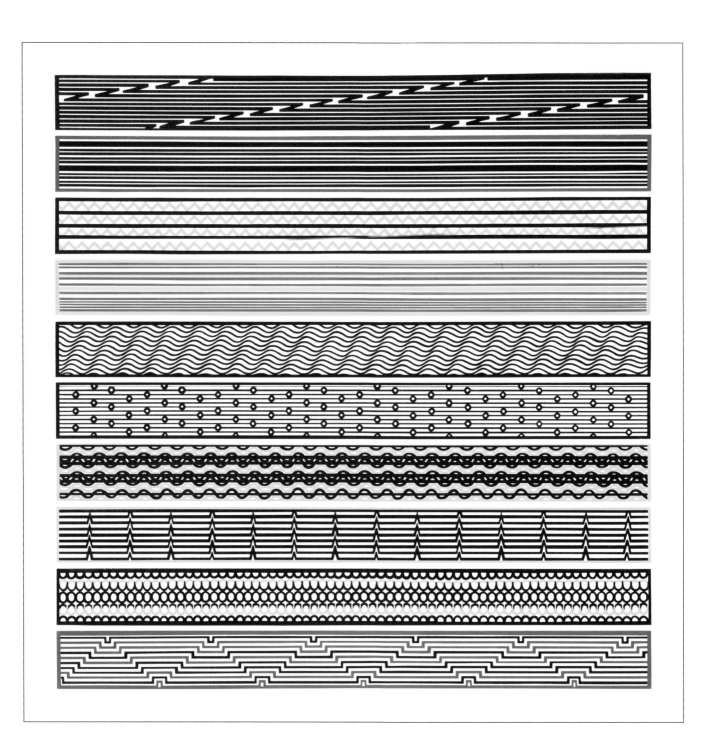

Lowest Expectations, 1996

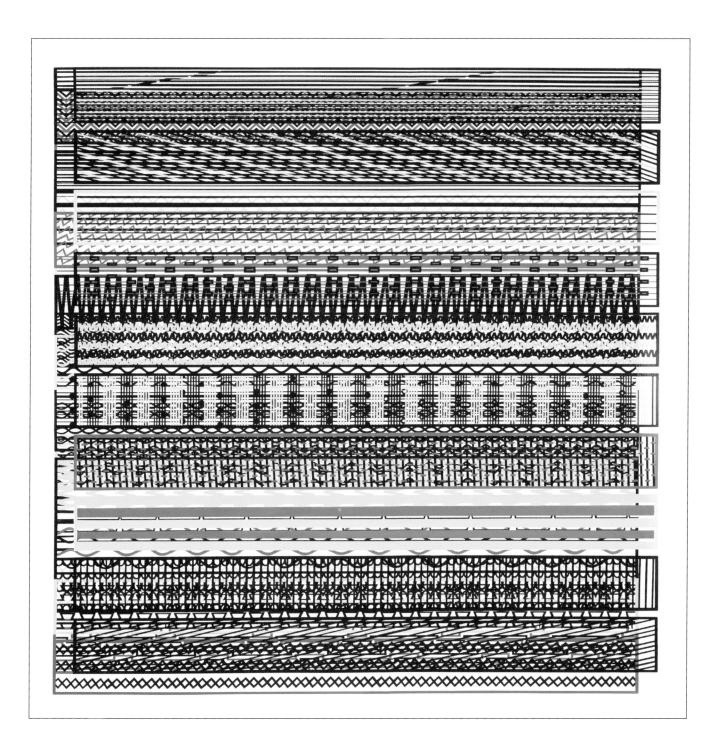

6th Lowest Expectations,1997

Delete all memories
Flatten all buildings
Fill all rivers with concrete

Proposal, 2001

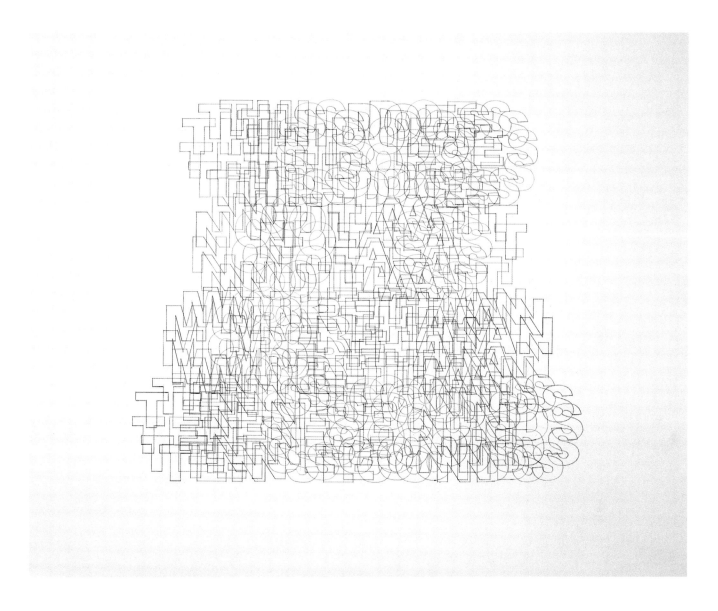

This Does Not Last More Than Ten Seconds, 2001

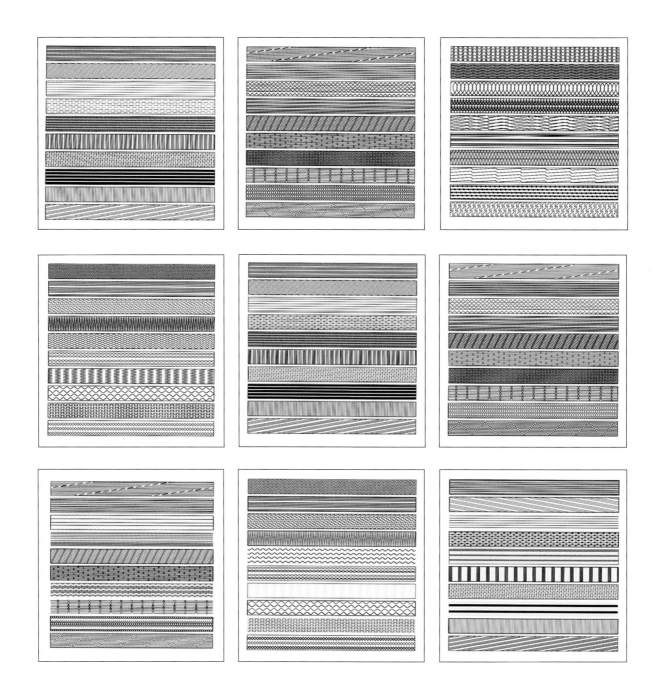

1st–6th Low, Lower and Lowest Expectations, 1996–97

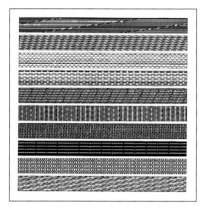
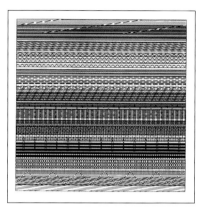
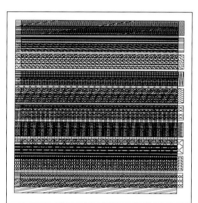
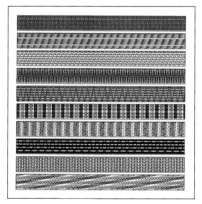
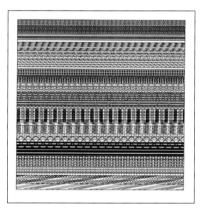
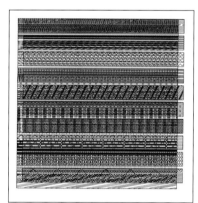
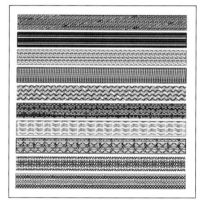
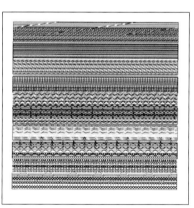
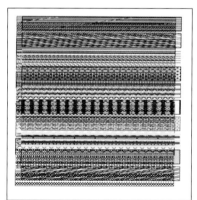

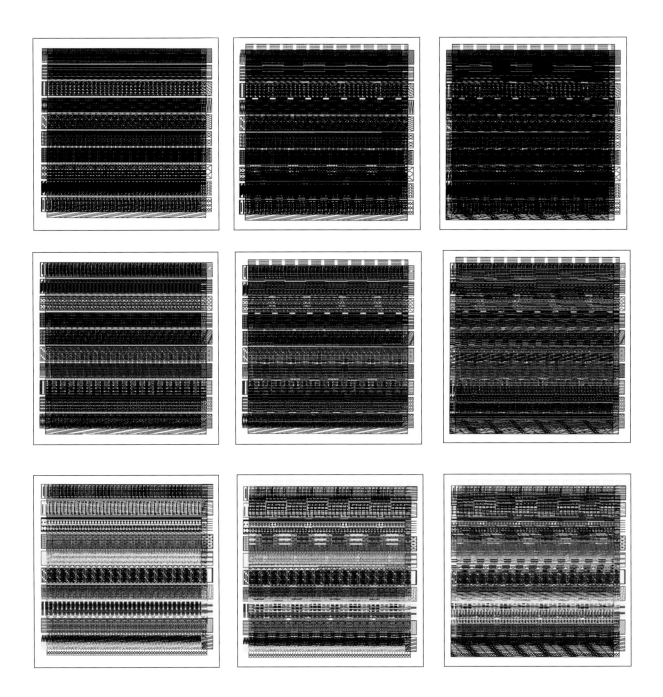

7th–12th Low, Lower and Lowest Expectations, 1996–97

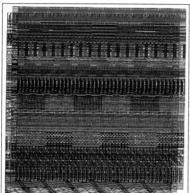 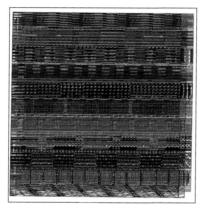 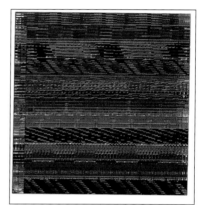

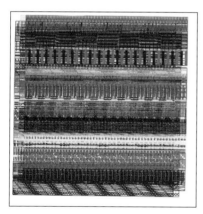 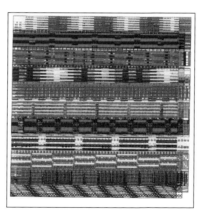 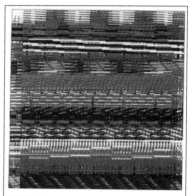

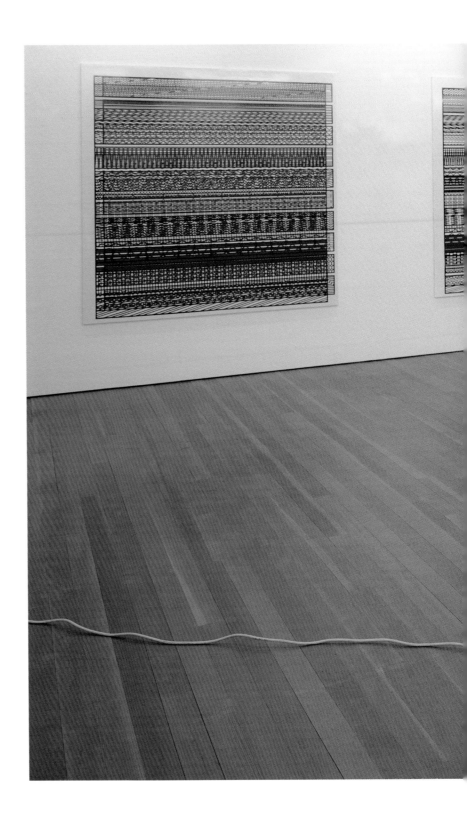

Installation view, The Foundation,
Ursula Blickle Stiftung, Kraichtal, Germany,
21 February–21 March 1999

A Couple of Differences
between Thinking and Feeling

Fairhurst has worked in three dimensions from the start, from the performative to the solid, from paper through to bronze and back again. His relation to the sculptural object is fascinating because the more solid a piece, the more funny and weightless it becomes. When transient – the artist himself on stage, for instance – the burden of humour takes on a weighty character. The very existence of an extremely large cartoon gorilla in the landscape can so readily dematerialise as a result of its own absurd fact, yet the gorilla moves between its role as object and image to become suggestive of arrested movement and silent groans.

Fairhurst is easily associated with the image of a gorilla. It populates his early cartoon drawings of man and beast in unlikely – sometimes comic, sometimes melancholic – pratfalls. The video *A Cheap and Ill-Fitting Gorilla Suit* (1995) shows a figure jumping up and down in a gorilla costume that sheds newspaper stuffing until eventually the artist himself is revealed naked. There were also the early appearances where Fairhurst, dressed as a gorilla, acted out sculptural poses, except in *Pietà* (1996; p. 89) where the dead Christ is a naked Fairhurst lying across the gorilla's lap.

The 'endism' of postmodernism was liberated by the super-dramatic imagery of British art at the beginning of the 1990s, and it made for a particularly powerful moment. It marked a movement from the aesthetic of minimalism to fulsome grandeur, and from the impossibility of picturing anything without recourse to the surface, to the introduction of drama and vanitas of an almost Victorian 'end of pier' dimension, with Damien Hirst's work, in particular. But it was never really any of that for Fairhurst, even if the give and take and the use of quotation, forever in his work – from extreme to meaninglessness, something or nothing, pattern and pull, more till it is not seen, and so on – mean a battle between the ascendency of grand subject and the impossibility of expression.

Left: A Couple of Differences between Thinking and Feeling, 2000–4

Untitled, 1994

The Birth of Consistency, 2004

He was part of the first artistic group to be characterised early on, in Britain anyway, as collective creators of work. The character of the gorilla was similar to that of Fairhurst himself who played up a combination of clown and fall guy. The body is the artist and yet the artist is not the thing exactly, and so Fairhurst holds onto his part as a sometimes reluctant performer in a production that is still somehow separate from him.

Untitled, 1994

At some point, the figure has left the loose and smelly suit to be cast in bronze. In the large bronze gorillas, the distinct lack of pomposity, combined with a hitherto unseen level of scale and gravitas, means a particularly timely relation between the un- real, the abject and the monumental. The gorilla plays less of a game here and becomes a thing. Not moving around, he, or it, is frozen, huge, suspended in relation to space and place. Not so funny. You can imagine that the gorilla made consistently over the years

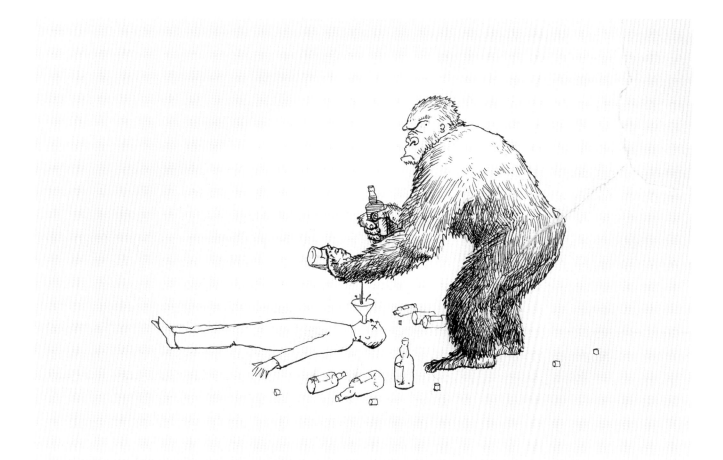

Untitled, 1992

continues to act for Fairhurst as a presence, something timeless that really can exist in the otherwise arbitrary world of rearranged two dimensions and perpetual reproduction.

Even more sad, vulnerable and touching than King Kong, these two-dimensional and three-dimensional constructions are a caricature in every way. It is hard for a sculpture to be funny in its very real self, for something monumental, permanent and heavy to carry anything more than pathos. Fairhurst's gorillas are part of a range of existence – heavy made light by reality and light made heavy through

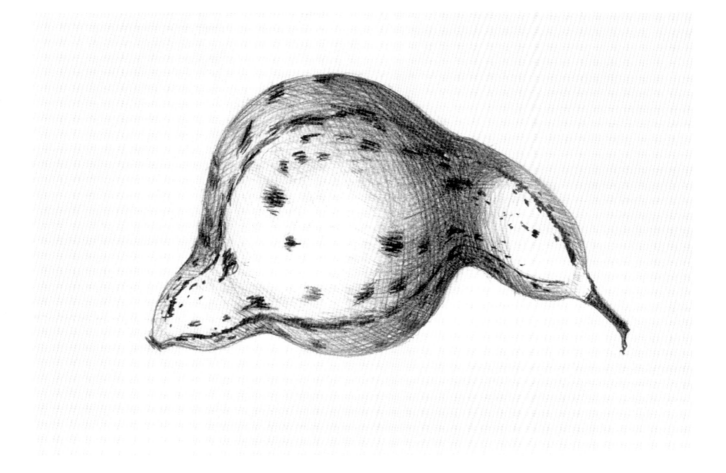

Above: Inflated, 1997
Left: Undone, 2004

Untitled, 2002

intense looking until the actuality of a figure becomes invisible. The gorilla parked outside on incongruous green parkland grass is huge, ineffectual in its relation to time, but with the constancy of inertia. They are, one might say, 'gentlegorillas' rather than gentlemen. In *The Birth of Consistency* (2004; p. 69), a gorilla looks at its own reflection in a pond, which it lifts, like a cruet set, to its face. This sculpture, like Narcissus, melds together figure and landscape. The gorillas encapsulate the beginning of the troubled and awkward state of being and the loss of an idiot's perceived peaceful existence – his at-oneness with nature.

The free-standing, chunky, jokey, choppy sea-surfaced, bronze-cast animal was never expected. The gorilla, with head off or head held underarm, or the gorilla crawling and walking upright, is successful in spite of its ridiculous self. As Fairhurst said: 'I wanted to make a classical sculpture which has the lightness of a cartoon…A solid object cannot look like it might just disappear if you stopped thinking about it but a cartoon seems light enough that it might just do that.'

Untitled, 2007

Untitled, 1994

Untitled, 1991

Untouched, 2004

A Couple of Differences between Thinking and Feeling II, 2003

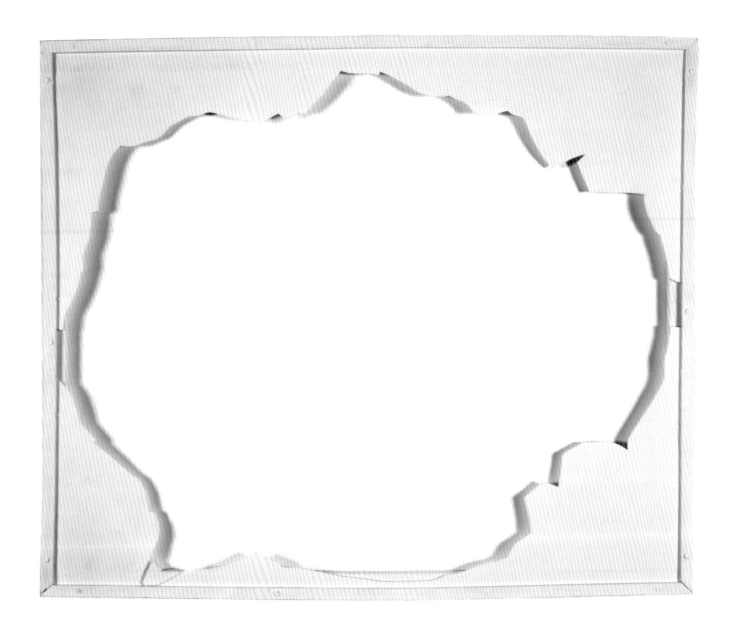

Mysterious Movement of the Wind, 2005

Mysterious Movement of the Wind, 2005

The Problem with Banana Skins Divided/Inverted, 1998

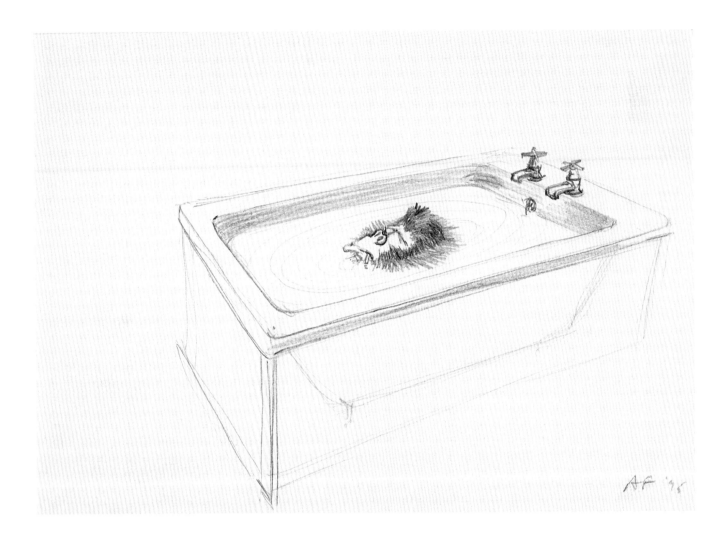

Untitled, 1995
Right: I'm Sorry, and I Won't Do It Again, 2004

Right: Pietà, 1996

Underdone/ Overdone Paintings

Numbered one to thirty, this series of paintings depicts a primeval forest, hallucinogenic rows of trees built up by and through repeated layers of colour separation. While not as systematic as the computer paintings *Low, Lower and Lowest Expectations*, the *Underdone/Overdone Paintings* crowd out almost completely any possibility of interpretation. The pictorial structures found in nature remain. Intensely amassed in a tonal, photographic sense, the red, blue and yellow trees remind, over and over again, that anything is able to work in relation to the structure of nature. A strong love and understating of natural form are important and evident in all Fairhurst's work. He reinforces the famous parallel between the artifice of nature and art itself.

It is hard to find a Fairhurst image that does not have some relationship to nature, and not just that, but also to the countryside, British landscape, trees, and the woods. 'Long live the weeds and the wilderness yet,' wrote Gerard Manley Hopkins in his poem *Inversnaid*. The Englishman Fairhurst planted trees, read about nature and photographed himself in its midst, needing to experience and understand its poetry and its philosophy. Fairhurst's work reflects the pull between the knowledge that experience is constructed, and the enjoyment of landscape for both possible and impossible reasons.

Whether tangled wood or calm copse, such a representation of a romantic idea, jettisoned long ago, is, for Fairhurst, still attractive. These silk-screens in red, blue, and yellow are simple and touching. But he insisted that 'they were meant to be blocked', in order to gain so many shifting, unfixed, transient views. Fairhurst is again here on perpetual standby, in the middle of the possible realisation of an image; he is a selfless speculator with a nagging intelligence, and pictures something only in order to prove

Left: Underdone/Overdone Painting No.1, 1998

its ultimate instability. Through the process of printing, and the repeats and shifts of colour, detail and emphasis, the image soon loses all point and meaning, and Fairhurst exposes not only a tendency towards repetition, but also the undermining of visual relevance that comes as a result of this.

The image here is immediately abstract, in the same way Mondrian's images were abstracted from nature. Yet, as Fairhurst insisted, it lacks Mondrian's 'incredible dogmatic optimism'. Fairhurst also said he wanted to refer to the paintings of Rothko in this series: to the accumulation of colour and the way the paint stops and starts in its consistent relation to the edge. Using a simple photographic scene, each of the pictures, paintings, or prints, is held within a margin or frame. But, moved by Mondrian's impressionistic break up, the result is something like a print made at the very beginning of an undergraduate course. The mesh of conflicting print, tree on tree, upside down, on top, always underneath, in blue, red, and yellow, with sleek trunks, makes a psychedelic image held within the frame. It starts out as a pretty generic glade, into which it is possible to take just one step. The tree trunks are rendered crudely, abject and unseductive, while the grid soon undermines the work consciously and unconsciously until there ceases to be a distinction between the two, and it all returns to no meaning.

A pivotal artist in his insistence on never settling down to moment and meaning, Fairhurst's collective imagery remains perversely gentle in its sophistication. Working through the range of possibilities within the series, the *Underdone/Overdone Paintings* bring out exactly that 'underdoing' and 'overdoing' that the display of them as a collective mass served to reinforce. They were originally presented as a frieze across two walls at Sadie Coles HQ, a wall of vision on a grid, with a drummer employed to play a random, unscored tattoo for an hour each day. Through its repetitiveness and the impossibility of escape for the viewer, the sound undoubtedly contributed to the cumulative sense of meaninglessness and confusion the paintings produce.

Left: Underdone/Overdone Painting No. 3, 1998

Whether passing through, building up, or taking away with a back to front reduction, the relationship to print is crucial. The linear photographic 'place' in strong colour forced through the silk-screen is reminiscent of posters on the wall in a 1960s adolescent's bedroom. The image will remain up there till it is no longer seen. The simple way in which the photographic image disintegrates is innocent and flows against a tide of random digital manipulation. Fairhurst uses media for its own formal self and there is no surreal construction, no making of otherness here. In fact, whether 'adding' with paint or 'taking away' with collage, the sense remains of a generation at Goldsmiths educated in the notion that different media can say different things effectively in their own way.

Above: Man with Dream Colours, 1992
Left: Mnemonic Table, 2004

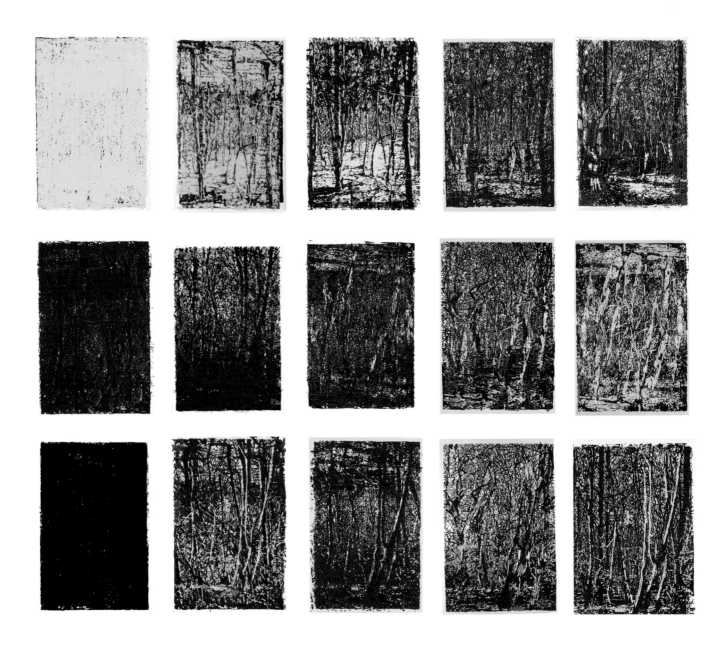

Top left to bottom right: Underdone/Overdone Paintings Nos. 1–30, 1998

Right: Installation view, The Missing Link, Sadie Coles HQ,
London, 28 October–28 November 1998

Underdone/Overdone Painting No.5, 1998

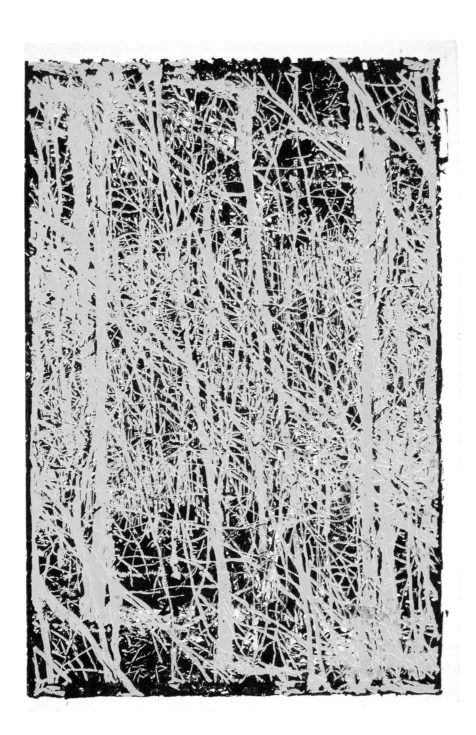

Underdone/Overdone Painting No. 6, 1998

Underdone/Overdone Painting No. 10, 1998

Underdone/Overdone Painting No. 13, 1998

Underdone/Overdone Painting No. 26, 1998

Underdone/Overdone Painting No. 30, 1998

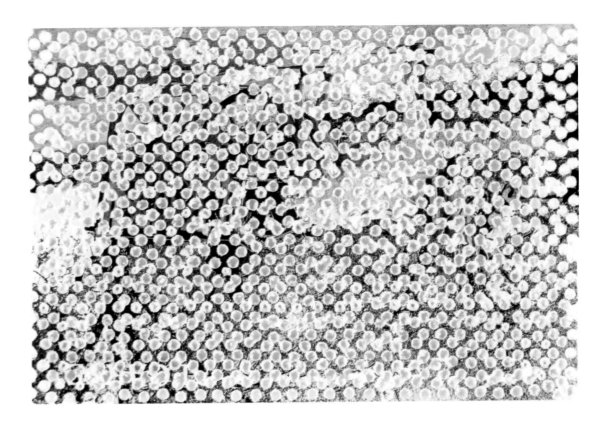

Portugal – Drilled, 1996

Magazine, All Body and Text Removed

Fairhurst has made collage the very beginning and ultimate end of his work. It is there from the very early drilled, punched photographs and postcard images, with the surfaces rhythmically punctured by processions of plastic tags, through to the magazine pages, and the bus stop and billboard advertising. From working backwards, cutting pages to hang three-dimensionally, the relationship between the world and photography, print, image, and text is so integrated, so embedded, that in a way all art-making is directly or indirectly a form of collage. The paintings in the last show have collaged elements brought to the same surface, while the work with advertising – the varying degrees of layer, depth, and arrangement of two-dimensional material – betrays a perpetual giving and taking away from a state of zero. Cutting back, the dignity of out-line merges with the push of hand, and deadpan solid colour is surrounded by blurred, bright lights. There is something of Francis Picabia's relationship to glamour, with his move between transgressive but lovely pictures of women, and nonetheless conceptually clear ruminations on the mechanisms of language.

Collage uses something that is already there to make something else. By taking something away it makes more, but by adding it also makes a difference. *A Magazine – Everything Removed Except 1cm Border* (2005; p. 114), is exactly that: a structure now so collapsed that it is a limp arabesque of coloured, gathered ribbon, a lantern of relief. *Ten Pages from a Magazine, Body and Text Removed* (2007; pp. 132–33) is also exactly that: it is a formal, sculptural rendition with planes, layers, shadow, tears, and colour that makes up an almost purist graphic structure. The body is still there, backwards, shifting, changing, alive through gestures that make a flicker book of fundamental moves. So, rather than placing one thing with another in order to reveal something surreal, inventive, or new, Fairhurst, too much a member of his generation to believe in art as pure invention, creates a concentrated reality.

The figure outlined in *Bourjois* (2006; p. 129) is posed, or poised, on top of and behind a set of stepping-stones cut from the outline of absented text. You know what is being said, but the shiny finish of advertising and fashion, touched-up lip-synch, lipstick, or lip outline (a sign for the cosmetic 'houses' of New York, Paris, and London), is turned into a greater, truer symbolic version of graphic events. Décollage – ripping, tearing paper from the poster site – leaves the modern glow of antiquated nostalgia. Here Fairhurst cuts with precision, using the scalpel to make clinical incisions into the body of graphic expectation. The result is always of the moment and never retrospectively composed in terms of time. The action here is sculptural, chipping away at the surface until Fairhurst reveals the graphic template beneath. Surrounded by diffuse lights, the figure that has been cut back into reveals a complex view. The fine outline of the hand makes an almost musical play, while the language of rediscovered Pop plays with formal completion.

Fairhurst has been taking the figure out of the equation for a very long time. Cutting back reveals the outline of the person beneath. He is a bit of a realist in the sense of his recognition of inevitable disaster and doom. Despite a career of getting rid of the person, it is, in the case of *Billboard, Everything but the Outline Blacked-In* (2003; pp. 116–17) or *Billboard, Everything but the Outline Whited-Out* (2004; pp. 118–19), always there, but reduced in detail to the very bones of context, in a calm way that implies there is no need to digress.

Fairhurst uses collage to expose depths of negative and positive space. The bare bones make a reference to what is already there: to historical imagery, to what makes something work, to the way it always has been, to picture making, advertising, painting, photography, fact and fiction. Fairhurst positions himself in the middle of this discussion. By cutting back, and through, he takes the surface sheen off a possibly perfect position to analyse the reality. The image can be obliterated, yet the idea and basic point remain. To repeat his mantra of giving and taking away, adding and subtracting, the artist stays in the middle as the reality, and the impossibility of image-making and the ineffectuality of art, battle it out. Instead of the notion of balance, a photo finish of idea and form, he says, through his work, that it is as difficult to make claims for a subject as it is disappointing to achieve.

St Paul's – Gridded & Punched, 1996

Working layer upon layer back through a magazine, Fairhurst exposes form and content. Billboards are huge. They are about mass consumption, about seeing something often, and *Six Billboards, Body and Text Removed* (2004; pp. 124–25) is a reminder of how very different this method of communication can be: bright, crass, shiny, reflective, water splashing, horizon dripping, cloudy, fresh, open, not one-to-one and lost in contemplation. There is no story, no true account, but fashion, with its baggage, here. The huge *24 Pages* (2007; pp. 134–35) alludes to a forward dimensionality, in the opposite way to a collapsing lantern. Here the pages project forward, but in a diminishing manner, becoming smaller when closer, showing hints of picture and pattern. A concertina of ever-expanding possibility, they emerge in a way that is to be celebrated. The magazine becomes as bare a skeleton as the 'for sale' sign. But the luxury of the modern belief that the artist can really transform, depart from, or shift reality, if only very briefly, is resolutely stamped on by such delicate and revealing pieces.

Faces – All Text & Graphics Removed, 2000

Two Pages from a Magazine, Body and Text Removed, 2003

Three Pages from a Magazine, Body and Text Removed, 2003
Overleaf left: A Magazine – Everything Removed Except 1 cm Border, 2005
Overleaf right: A Magazine with the Body and Text Removed, 2004

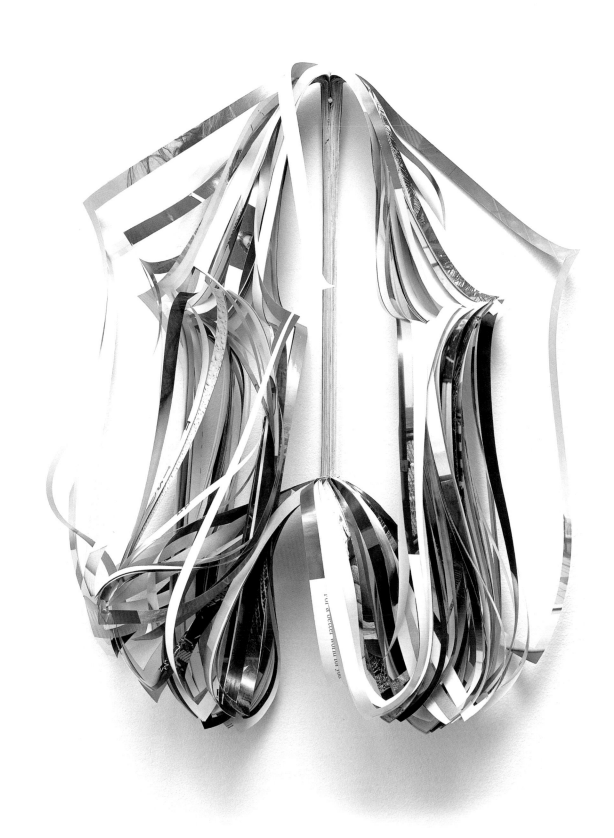

Billboard, Everything but the Outline Blacked-In, 2003

Billboard, Everything but the Outline Whited-Out, 2004

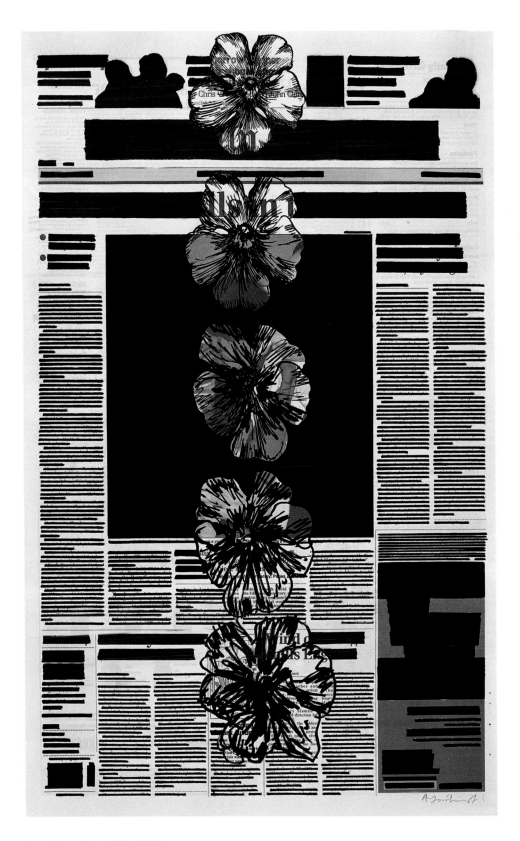

Unwritten (May 18th), 2001

One Year of the News (1st January–31 December 2003), 2004
Following pages: Five Billboards, Body and Text Removed, 2004
Six Billboards, Body and Text Removed, 2004

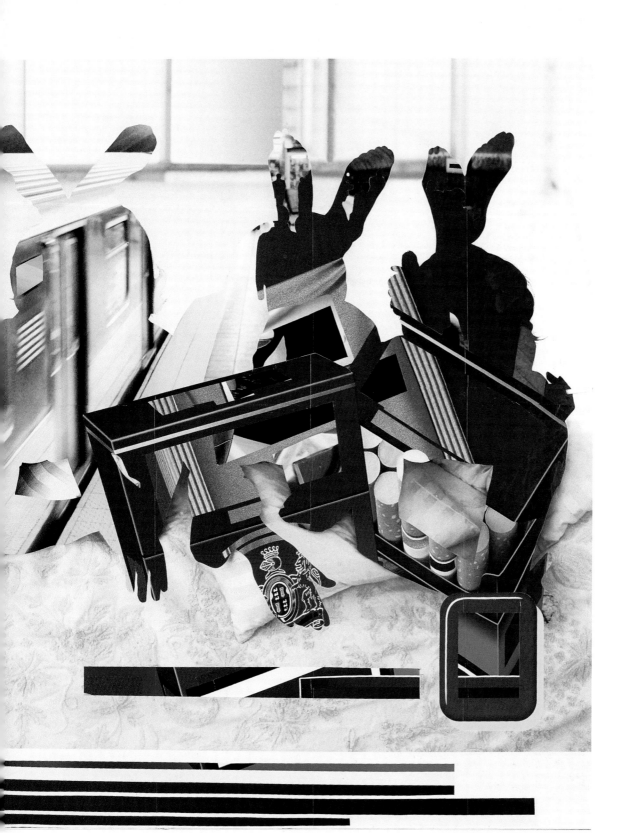

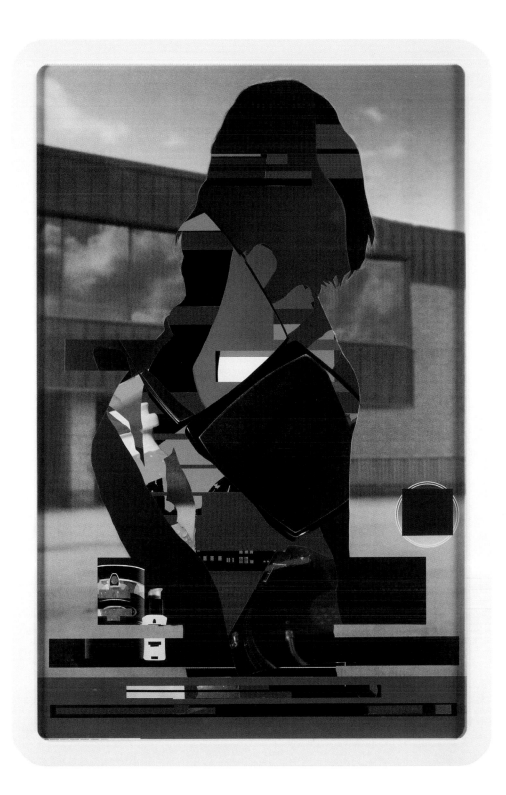

Angel, 2006

Still, 2006

Powder, 2006

Bourjois, 2006

Ten Pages from a Magazine, Body and Text Removed, 2007

Ten Pages from a Magazine, Body and Text Removed, 2007

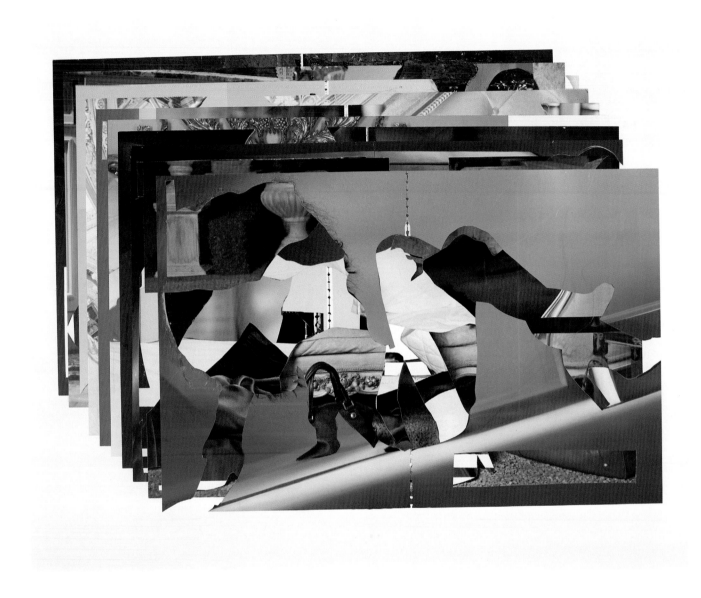

Ten Pages from a Magazine, Body and Text Removed, 2007

Ten Pages from a Magazine, Body and Text Removed, 2007

24 Pages, 2007

24 Pages, 2007

Deep Brain Stimulation, 2007

Acknowledgments

Sadie Coles HQ would like to thank all of the curators, collaborators and galleries of Angus Fairhurst. Their support and involvement are warmly appreciated both in the making of this book and for the exhibitions they made with the artist. Thank you to Steven Adamson, Paul Andriesse, Pantelis Arapinis, Charles Asprey, Chris Bell, Pierre Bismuth, Ursula Blickle, Bruno Brunnet, Angela Bulloch, Mat Collishaw, Thomas Dane, Ian Davenport, Richard Flood, Douglas Fogle, Márcia Fortes, Carl Freedman, Anya Gallaccio, Liam Gillick, Jorg Grimm, Nicole Hackert, Andrew Hale, Steve Hanson, Philipp Haverkampf, Lothar Hempel, Georg Herold, Damien Hirst, Gary Hume, Giovanni Intra, Jay Jopling, Stefan Kalmar, Georg Kargl, Paul Kasmin, Anton Kern, Rungwe Kingdon, Udo Kittleman, Claude Koenig, Michael Landy, Abigail Lane, Lala Meredith-Vula, Harland Miller, Gregor Muir, Sarah Lucas, Stephen Park, Richard Patterson, Simon Patterson, Barbara Polla, Fiona Rae, Sir Norman Rosenthal, Karsten Schubert, Billee Sellman, Dorothea Strauss, Tom Trevor, Alessandra Vilaça, Clarrie Wallis, Gillian Wearing, Max Wigram, Cerith Wyn Evans, Marta Ybarra and so many others.

We are grateful to Sir Nicholas Serota for his perceptive introduction to the catalogue, to James Cahill for his overview of Angus Fairhurst's oeuvre, and especially to Sacha Craddock for her intimate reflection on time spent with the artist and his work. Thanks are also due to Keith Pointing and Philip Wilson for their commitment to this publication.

Sadie Coles and Pauline Daly give personal thanks to Sally Fairhurst and Charles Fairhurst for their unwavering support of the book and exhibition. And to Angus, thank you from all of us and more, for your company, your art, and your ideas.

ANGUS FAIRHURST
Biography

Educated
1985–86 Canterbury Art College, Kent
1986–89 Goldsmith's College, London

Selected Solo Exhibitions
2009   Angus Fairhurst, Arnolfini,
         Bristol, UK
2008   Sadie Coles HQ, London
2006   Grimm Fine Art, Amsterdam
         Unwit, Paul Kasmin Gallery,
         New York (NY)
2005   *Notnot*, Vacio 9, Madrid
2004   *Unwork*, Contemporary Fine Arts,
         Berlin
         Dysuniversal, Georg Kargl, Vienna
2002   *Angus Fairhurst*, Alphadelta Gallery
         – Artio Gallery, Athens
2001   *This Does Not Last More Than One
         Second*, Spacex Gallery,
         Exeter, UK
         More or Less Angus Fairhurst,
         Sadie Coles HQ, London
         Angus Fairhurst More or Less,
         China Art Objects Gallery, Los
         Angeles (CA)
         *This Does Not Last More Than Ten
         Seconds*, Kunsthalle St Gallen, St
         Gallen, Switzerland
1999   *The Trouble with Comedy*,
         Contemporary Fine Arts, Berlin Art
         Fair, Berlin
         The Foundation, Ursula Blickle
         Stiftung, Kraichtal, Germany (cat.)
         and Kunsthalle St Gallen, St
         Gallen, Switzerland
1998   *The Missing Link*, Sadie Coles HQ,
         London
         Standing Stock Still, Anton Kern
         Gallery, New York (NY)
         Odd-Bod Photography (with Sarah
         Lucas), Sadie Coles HQ, London
         and Kolnischer Kunstverein,
         Cologne, Germany
1997   *Stand Still and Rot*, Contemporary
         Fine Arts, Berlin
1996   *Low Lower Lowest*, Jay Jopling/
         White Cube, London
         The Artist Has Left (with

Lothar Hempel), Anton Kern Gallery,
New York (NY)
A Cheap and Ill-Fitting Relationship,
Paul Andriesse Gallery, Amsterdam
*A False Dawn on the Road to
Personal and Artistic Freedoms*,
Ridinghouse Editions, London
1994   *Gallery Connections*,
         Karsten Schubert Ltd., London
         Drawings and Cartoons,
         71 Hartham Road, London
1993   *All Evidence of Man Removed*,
         Karsten Schubert Ltd., London
1992   *Man Abandoned by Space*, Galerie
         Analix, Geneva, Switzerland (cat.)
         Etats spécifiques, Musée des
         Beaux-Arts André Malraux, Le
         Havre, France (cat.)
1991   *Some Went Mad, Some Ran Away*,
         Karsten Schubert Ltd., London
1990   *You in Mind*, Karsten Schubert Ltd.,
         London

Selected Group Exhibitions
2008   *You Dig the Tunnel, I'll Hide the
         Soil*, White Cube, London
2006   *Nothing but Pleasure*, Bawag
         Foundation, Vienna
         Dada's Boys, The Fruitmarket
         Gallery, Edinburgh
         Survivor, Bortolami Dayan,
         New York (NY)
         Dark, Museum Boijmans
         van Beuningen, Rotterdam,
         The Netherlands
         *In the Darkest Hour There May Be
         Light: Works from Damien Hirst's
         Murderme Collection*,
         Serpentine Gallery, London
2005   *Bazar de Verāo*, Galeria Fortes
         Vilaça, São Paulo, Brazil
         Cross Section, Paul Kasmin Gallery,
         New York (NY)
         Vertigo, Sudeley Castle,
         Winchcombe, Gloucestershire,
         UK
         Y[oung] B[ritish] A[rtists]
         Criss-Crossed, Galleri Kaare
         Bernsten, Oslo
         Out of the Melting Pot,

Dexia Banque Internationale à
Luxembourg, Luxembourg

2004 *Summer Exhibition*, Royal Academy,
London (cat.)
Collage, Bloomberg SPACE, London
57th Aldeburgh Festival,
Contemporary British Sculpture
at Snape (Angus Fairhurst,
Damien Hirst, Sarah Lucas),
Snape, UK
Drunkenmasters (Angus
Fairhurst, Liam Gillick, Cerith
Wyn-Evans), Galeria Fortes
Vilaça, São Paulo, Brazil
In-A-Gadda-Da-Vida (with
Sarah Lucas and Damien Hirst),
Tate Britain, London (cat.)

2003 *Trickfilm*, Buchmann Galerie,
Cologne, Germany
Sterling Stuff: Fifty Sculptors,
Sigurjon Olafsson Museum,
Reykjavik and Royal Academy
of Arts, London
In Retrospect: Thirty Sculptors,
Gallery Pangolin, Chalford, UK

2002 *Sterling Stuff: Fifty Sculptors*,
Gallery Pangolin, Chalford, UK
Generator, Spacex Gallery,
Exeter, UK
Iconoclast: Beyond the Image Wars,
ZKM, Karlsruhe, Germany (cat.)
'Why Bother?' The Burger King
Exhibition, Burger King, London
(cat.)
Man in the Middle, Sammlung
Deutsche Bank, Frankfurt am Main,
Germany
The Unblinking Eye: Lens-Based
Work from the IMMA Collection, Irish
Museum of Modern Art, Dublin

2001 *Casino 2001*, S.M.A.K. Gent,
Belgium (cat.)
Open Plan P3 – The Marathon
(curated by Sofia and Dimitria
Vamiali), Alphadelta Gallery – Artio
Gallery, Athens (cat.)
Animations, P.S.1 Contemporary Art
Center, New York (NY)
Alternative Currents, The Mac,
McKinney Avenue Contemporary,

Dallas (TX)
Century City: Art and Culture in
the Modern Metropolis,
Tate Modern, London (cat.)
Lens and Paper – the Beauty
of Intimacy, Gemeentemuseum,
The Hague and tour to Staatliche
Kunsthalle Baden-Baden and
Museum Haus am Waldsee, Berlin
(cat.)

2000 *Apocalypse,* The Royal Academy,
London (cat.)
Video-Vibe, British School in
Rome, Rome (cat.)
00, Barbara Gladstone Gallery, New
York (NY) (cat.)
Body Beautiful, Galerie Jennifer
Flay, Paris
Puerile 69: Angus Fairhurst, Michael
Landy, Sarah Lucas, Gillian
Wearing, The Living Art Museum,
Reykjavik (cat.)
About Collage, Tate Liverpool,
Liverpool, UK (cat.)
Sanssouci Oder: Die Kunst Der
Entsorgung, Badischer Kunstverein,
Karlsruhe, Germany (cat.)
The Anagrammatical Body, ZKM
Centre for Media Art and Technology,
Karlsruhe, Germany
Sex and the British, Galerie
Thaddeaus Ropac, Salzburg, Austria,
and Paris
Psycho, Art and Anatomy,
Anne Faggionato, London

1999 *Art Lovers*, Liverpool
Biennial, Liverpool, UK
The Anagrammatical Body,
Neue Landesmuseum, Graz,
Austria

1998 *Thinking Aloud*, Kettle's Yard,
Cambridge and tour to Camden Arts
Centre, London (cat.)
Maximum Diversity, Galerie
Krinzinger in den Benger Fabrik,
Bregenezand Atelierhaus der
Akademie der Bildenden Kunste,
Vienna (cat.)
Crossings, Kunst Zum Horen und
Sehen, Kunsthalle, Vienna (cat.)

(touring exhibition)

1997 *Dimensions Variable*, British Council
Touring Exhibition (cat.)
Package Holiday, Hydra Workshops,
Hydra, Greece (cat.)
Other Men's Flowers, The
British School in Rome, Rome
From Figure to Object,
Karsten Schubert Ltd. and
Frith Street Gallery, London (cat.)

1996 *Plastic*, Arnolfini Gallery,
Bristol and tour to Walsall
Museum and Art Gallery,
Walsall, UK (cat.)
Full House, Kunstmuseum,
Wolfsburg, Germany
Domestic Violence, Rhona Hoffmann
Gallery, Chicago (IL)
*A Small Shifting Sphere of Serious
Culture*, ICA, London and tour
(video programme)
Other Men's Flowers, Aurel
Scheibler, Cologne, Germany

1995 *Brilliant! New Art from London*,
Walker Art Centre, Minneapolis (MI),
touring to Contemporary Art
Museum, Houston (TX) (cat.)
Corpus Delicti,
Portalen, Copenhagen (cat.)

1994 *Karaoke Football*, Portikus
No. 58, Frankfurt am Main, Germany
Some Went Mad, Some Ran Away,
Serpentine Gallery, London,
touring to Nordic Arts Centre,
Helsinki; Kunstverein, Hanover,
Germany; Museum of Contemporary
Art, Chicago (IL) (cat.)
Not Self Portrait, Karsten Schubert
Ltd., London

1993 *Privacy*, Opos, Milan, Italy (cat.)
Other Men's Flowers, Factual
Nonsense, London

1992 *Twenty Fragile Pieces*, Galerie
Analix, Geneva, Switzerland (cat.)
Etats Spécifiques, Musée des
Beaux-Arts André Malraux, Le
Havre, France (cat.)
Mat Collishaw, Angus Fairhurst,
Abigail Lane, Viafarini, Milan,
Italy (cat.)

1991 *Gambler*, Building One,
London (cat.)

1988 *Freeze*, PLA Building,
London (cat.)

Performances

2001 *L▮▮▮▮▮▮▮s*
Kunsthalle St Gallen,
Switzerland
L▮▮▮▮▮▮▮s
Exeter Phoenix

1999 *Lowest Expectations*, The
Scala, London
Lowest Expectations, British Council,
Cologne, Germany
Lower Expectations, Ursula Bickle
Stiftung, Kraichtal, Germany

1998 *Low Expectations*, Buro Friedrich,
Berlin
Low Expectations, Flex, Vienna

1997 *Top Ten Expectations*, ICA, London
Low Expectations, Cable Factory,
Helsinki

1996 *Low Expectations*, Dean Street,
London
Lexopewctations, Anton Kern
Gallery, New York (NY)

1995 *Low Expectations*, Brixton
Academy, London
Low Expectations, 56a Clerkenwell
Road, London

FULL LIST OF WORKS

*My House Fell Down but Now I Can
See the Stars*
2001
Ink and pencil on paper
40.6 x 54.6 cm
Unique
p. 6

Unseen, 2004
Bronze
10 x 251 x 178 cm
Installation view, *Dysuniversal*, Georg
Kargl, Vienna,
11 November 2004–9 January 2005
Edition of three
p. 10

*Three Double Pages from a Magazine,
Body and Text Removed*
2004
Cut-out magazine on paper
30 x 45.3 cm
Unique
p. 14

Rainbow's End (inside)
2000
Pencil, ink and collage on card
21 x 29.5 cm
Unique
p. 15

Marcel Duchamp (1887–1968)
*Étant donnés: 1. la chute d'eau / 2. le gaz
d'éclairage*
1946–66
Mixed-media assemblage
242.6 x 177.8 cm
Unique
p. 16

*Things That Don't Work Properly/
Things That Never Stop* (video stills)
1998
Video
Edition of three
p. 17

Primary Forest 5
1998
Ink on paper
221 x 152.4 cm
Unique
p. 22

Samuel Palmer (1805–81)
The Magic Apple Tree
1830
Pen and indian ink, watercolour on paper
34.9 x 27.3 cm
Unique
p. 23

Fata Morgana

Saen01
2007
Collage and acrylic paint on board
89 x 91 cm
Unique
p. 30

Saen02
2007
Collage and acrylic paint on board
74 x 91 cm
Unique
p. 33

Pala02
2007
Collage and acrylic paint on board
88 x 90 cm
Unique
p. 35

Schopfun
2008
Acrylic and silk-screen with
collage on canvas
250 x 335 x 3.2 cm
Unique
pp. 36–37

Lessons in Darkness
2008
Bronze
60 x 33 x 55 cm
Plinth: 100 x 60 x 60 cm
Edition of six
p. 38

Untitled (with Bird)
2007
Bronze
41 x 45 x 35 cm
Plinth: 81 x 45.5 x 55.2 cm
Edition of six
p. 39

Fata Morgana
2008
Acrylic and collage on canvas
250 x 335 x 3.2 cm
Unique
pp. 40–41

The Great Ecstasy
2008
Acrylic on resin
125 x 122 x 122 cm
Edition of two
p. 42

Epha
2008
Acrylic and chinagraph on canvas
61 x 46 x 3.2 cm
Unique
p. 43

Gree
2008
Acrylic and silk-screen with collage on
canvas
61 x 76 x 3.2 cm
Unique
p. 44

Eenp
2008
Acrylic and silk-screen with collage on
canvas
61 x 76 x 3.2 cm
Unique
p. 45

Enpa
2008
Acrylic and silk-screen with collage on
canvas
61 x 76 x 3.2 cm
Unique
p. 46

Installation views, Sadie Coles HQ, London,
21 February–29 March 2008
p. 47

Lowest Expectations

5th Lowest Expectations (detail)
1996
Enamel paint on aluminium panel
180 x 180 cm
Unique
p. 48

Low Expectations, Performance,
21 Dean Street, London,
26 November 1996
p. 50

Low Expectations
1996
Enamel paint on aluminium panel
180 x 180 cm
Unique
p. 52

6th Low Expectations
1997
Enamel paint on aluminium panel
180 x 180 cm
Unique
p. 53

Lower Expectations
1996
Enamel paint on aluminium panel
180 x 180 cm
Unique
p. 54

6th Lower Expectations
1997
Enamel paint on aluminium panel
180 x 180 cm
Unique
p. 55

Lowest Expectations
1996
Enamel paint on aluminium panel
180 x 180 cm
Unique
p. 56

6th Lowest Expectations
1997
Enamel paint on aluminium panel
180 x 180 cm
Unique
p. 57

Proposal
2001
Pencil on paper
60 x 80 cm
Unique
p. 58

This Does Not Last More Than Ten Seconds
2001
Pencil on paper
74.5 x 84.5 cm
Unique
p. 59

1st–6th Low, Lower and Lowest Expectations, 1996–97
pp. 60–61

7th–12th Low, Lower and Lowest Expectations, 1996–97
pp. 62–63

Installation view, *The Foundation*,
Ursula Blickle Stiftung, Kraichtal, Germany,
21 February–21 March 1999 pp. 64–65

A Couple of Differences between Thinking and Feeling

A Couple of Differences between Thinking and Feeling
2000
Cast bronze
210 x 173 x 132 cm
Edition of three
p. 66

Untitled
1994
Pencil on paper
29.7 x 21 cm
Unique
p. 68

The Birth of Consistency
2004
Resin and mirrored acrylic
91.4 x 300 x 152 cm
Edition of three
p. 69

Untitled
1994
Ink on paper
21 x 30 cm
Unique
p. 70

Untitled
1992
Pencil on paper
21 x 29.7 cm
Unique
p. 71

Undone
2004
Bronze
61 x 274 x 137 cm
Edition of three
p. 72

Inflated
1997
Pencil on paper
25.5 x 28 cm
Unique
p. 73

Untitled
2002
Ink on paper
Unique
p. 74

Untitled
2007
Bronze
41 x 45 x 35 cm
Edition of six
p. 76

Untitled
1994
Pencil on paper
29.7 x 21 cm
Unique
p. 77

Untitled
1991
Pencil on paper
21 x 29.7 cm
Unique
p. 78

Untouched
2004
Bronze and stainless steel
70 x 183 x 152.5 cm
Edition of three
p. 79

A Couple of Differences between Thinking and Feeling II
2003
Bronze
Figure: 165 x 140 x 105 cm
Arm: 31 x 120 x 67 cm
Edition of three
p. 81

Mysterious Movement of the Wind
2005
Bioresin
101.5 x 122 x 3.5 cm
Edition of three
p. 82

Mysterious Movement of the Wind
2005
Bioresin
101.5 x 122 x 3.5 cm
Edition of three
p. 83

The Problem with Banana Skins Divided/Inverted
1998
Polyurethane rubber
36 x 36 x 7 cm
Edition of ten
pp. 84–85

Untitled
1995
Pencil on paper
30 x 22 cm
Unique
p. 86

I'm Sorry, and I Won't Do It Again
2004
Bronze
34 x 22.5 x 11.5 cm
Edition of six
p. 87

Pietà
1996
Cibachrome print
248 x 183 cm
Edition of six
p. 89

Underdone/Overdone Paintings

Underdone/Overdone Painting No. 1
1998
Acrylic silk-screen on panel
90 x 60 cm
Unique
p. 90

Underdone/Overdone Painting No. 3
1998
Acrylic silk-screen on panel
90 x 60 cm
Unique
p. 92

Mnemonic Table, 2004
Table, flowerpots, ivy, honeysuckle,
bindweed bramble
109 x 188 x 71 cm
Installation view, *In-A-Gadda-Da-Vida*,
Tate Britain, London, 3 March–31 May 2004
p. 94

Man with Dream Colours
1992
Cibachrome prints on board with garment
attachments
(x4) 101 x 101 cm
p. 95

Underdone/Overdone Paintings Nos. 1–30,
1998
pp. 96–97

Installation view, *The Missing Link*, Sadie
Coles HQ, London, 28 October–28
November 1998
p. 99

Underdone/Overdone Painting No. 5
1998
Acrylic silk-screen on panel
90 x 60 cm
Unique
p. 100

Underdone/Overdone Painting No. 6
1998
Acrylic silk-screen on panel
90 x 60 cm
Unique
p. 101

Underdone/Overdone Painting No. 10
1998
Acrylic silk-screen on panel
90 x 60 cm
Unique
p. 102

Underdone/Overdone Painting No. 13
1998
Acrylic silk-screen on panel
90 x 60 cm
Unique
p. 103

Underdone/Overdone Painting No. 26
1998
Acrylic silk-screen on panel
90 x 60 cm
Unique
p. 104

Underdone/Overdone Painting No. 30
1998
Acrylic silk-screen on panel
90 x 60 cm
Unique
p. 105

Magazine, All Body and Text Removed

Portugal – Drilled
1996
Drilled postcard
10 x 15 cm
Unique
p. 106

St Paul's – Gridded & Punched
1996
Gridded and punched postcard
10 x 15 cm
Unique
p. 109

Faces - All Text & Graphics Removed
2000
Cut magazine page
145.5 x 111 cm
Unique
p. 111

*Two Pages from a Magazine, Body and
Text Removed*
2003
Cut-out magazine on paper
28.5 x 22.3 cm
Unique
p. 112

*Three Pages from a Magazine, Body and
Text Removed*
2003
Cut-out magazine on paper
29.8 x 22.4 cm
Unique
p. 113

*A Magazine – Everything Removed Except
1 cm Border*
2005
Cut magazine
Unique
p. 114

A Magazine with the Body and Text Removed
2004
Cut magazine
60 x 46 x 17 cm
Unique
p. 115

*Billboard, Everything but the Outline
Blacked-In*
2003
Billboard poster, acrylic paint, frame
336 x 600 cm
Unique
pp. 116–17

*Billboard, Everything but the Outline
Whited-Out*
2001
Billboard poster, acrylic paint, frame
336 x 600 cm
Unique
pp. 118–19

Unwritten (May 18th)
2001
Ink on newsprint on paper
59 x 41.5 cm
Unique
p. 120

One Year of the News (1st January–31 December 2003), 2004
Inkjet print on paper, 6 newspapers x 52 weeks, 12 panels
316 x 1976 cm
Installation view, *In-A-Gadda-Da-Vida*, Tate Britain, London, 3 March–31 May 2004
p. 121

Five Billboards, Body and Text Removed
2004
Collaged billboards posters
240 x 507 cm
Unique
pp. 122–23

Six Billboards, Body and Text Removed
2004
Collaged billboard posters
244 x 350 cm
Unique
pp. 124–25

Angel
2006
Collaged posters, custom made frame
189.9 x 130.2 cm
Unique
p. 126

Still
2006
Collaged posters, custom made frame
189.9 x 130.2 cm
Unique
p. 127

Powder
2006
Collaged posters, custom made frame
189.9 x 130.2 cm
Unique
p. 128

Bourjois
2006
Collaged poster, custom made frame
189.9 x 130.2 cm
Unique
p. 129

Ten Pages from a Magazine, Body and Text Removed
2007
Cut-out magazine on card
35 x 26 cm
Unique
p. 130

Ten Pages from a Magazine, Body and Text Removed
2007
Cut-out magazine on card
33 x 29 cm
Unique
p. 131

Ten Pages from a Magazine, Body and Text Removed
2007
Cut-out magazine on card
41 x 55 cm
Unique
p. 132

Ten Pages from a Magazine, Body and Text Removed
2007
Cut-out magazine on card
37.8 x 52.5 cm
Unique
p. 133

24 pages
2007
Cut-out magazine on card
73.7 x 68.6 cm
Unique
p. 134

24 pages
2007
Cut-out magazine on card
67.9 x 77.7 cm Unique
p. 135

Deep Brain Stimulation
2007
Collage
148 x 122 cm
Unique
p. 136

Covers and endpapers

Front cover
A Couple of Differences between Thinking and Feeling II
2003
Bronze
figure: 165 x 140 x 105 cm
arm: 31 x 120 x 67 cm
Edition of three

Back cover
Fata Morgana (detail)
2008
Acrylic and collage on canvas
250 x 335 x 3.2 cm
Unique

Title page
An Effortless Patch #1
1998
C-print on MDF
122 x 99 cm
Edition of three